P9-ELS-174

AUSTRALIAN PATCHWORK DESIGNS

A Step-by-Step Guide to Piecing, Quilting & Appliqué

AUSTRALIAN PATCHWORK DESIGNS

A Step-by-Step Guide to Piecing, Quilting & Appliqué

Margaret Rolfe

Sterling Publishing Co., Inc., New York

Published in 1986 by
Sterling Publishing Co., Inc.
Two Park Avenue
New York, N.Y. 10016

ISBN 0 8069 6356 5 Trade
        6354 9 Paperback

First published in Australia in 1985 as 'Australian Patchwork'
by Lloyd O'Neil Pty Ltd
This edition available in the United States and Canada only

Cover design: Zoë Gent-Murphy
Design and illustrations: Heather Jones
Typesetting: Betty Chapman
Photography: Mike Fisher

Typeset in Australia
Printed in Hong Kong through Bookbuilders Ltd

Acknowledgements: The publishers would like to thank the
Australian Women's Weekly for providing the photograph of
the author, and The Australiana General Store, Armadale,
Victoria, for lending items used in the photographs.

Contents

List of plates

Acknowledgements

I would like to express my gratitude to all my family and friends who helped in the making of this book.

My son Philip (then eleven) really began the whole thing by saying to me one day, "Mummy, why don't you make your designs into a book?" His own talent for design can be seen in the blocks for the **Wattle** and **Sturt's desert rose**. My other son Bernie contributed the **Gumnut** border design—and no Australian patchwork book would be complete without a gumnut somewhere!

I would like to thank Linda McGuire for her help and encouragement from the very beginning, and also for the beautiful work that she has contributed to be photographed. Judy Turner assisted, by generously sharing her enormous practical expertise in patchwork construction, as well as making many of the items featured in the book. Pamela Tawton has made this a richer and better book by allowing me to publish her beautiful designs for Australian wildflowers in the stained-glass technique. Beryl Hodges helped with perceptive proof reading, and also lent some of her lovely work to be pictured. Thanks also to Judy Edwards, Marjorie Coleman, Wendy Saclier and Anne Moten, whose original talents can be seen in the work that they have been willing to share in this book. Julie Filmer also lent some of her immaculate patchwork. I would like to thank my parents, Linda and Alex Poppins, and also Margaret O'Callaghan and Joan Fitzgerald for their practical help on numerous occasions. I am grateful to Dulcie Thompson and Barbara Goddard for lending their cushions to be photographed. My thanks to Pat and Warwick Wright for lending their books to me, and being so patient about their return.

Most of all I must thank my husband, Barry, for all his energetic and enthusiastic support, and also for his help in preparing the designs for publication. Without his help, this book would not exist.

Margaret Rolfe

A note on metrication

All measurements in this book are given using both metric and imperial units. For purposes of clarity and practicality the conversions are not exact, but care has been taken to round the imperial figures to their closes metric equivalent.

Glossary

Appliqué The term used to describe a patchwork method in which one fabric is applied or put on to another fabric. Usually there is a background fabric, and shapes of other fabrics are cut out and sewn onto the background. Applique is especially suited to curved and naturalistic shapes.

Batting The layer of padding between the top and the back of the quilt 'sandwich'. The most readily available kind of batting is made from polyester, but it is also possible to use batting made from cotton (sometimes called wadding), or carded wool.

Bias Refers to the direction on fabric at 45° to the grain (see *Grain* below). Strips of fabric cut in the direction of the bias have many uses in patchwork for finishing edges, and can also be used to cover raw edges in bias applique (see *Bias applique* below). You can also buy ready-made bias binding, referred to in the book as *purchased bias binding*. Note that this purchased bias binding is described by its folded width, not the width of the original bias strip.

Bias appliqué A form of applique in which the raw edges of the pieces to be applied are covered by narrow folded strips of bias. When the bias strips are black, this is called a *stained-glass* technique, as it has the appearance that this name suggests.

Block This is the basic unit of patchwork designs. Blocks are mostly square units, though they need not necessarily be so. A block can be used on its own to make a cushion (pillow) or small item, or several of the same block (or various blocks the same size) can be used together to make a quilt or larger item.

Grain Refers to the direction in which the threads run in a piece of fabric. The threads run both vertically and horizontally (the warp and weft). To 'match the grain' means to match either of these directions. It is important to the finished appearance of patchwork that, whenever possible, the grain of the fabric is kept in a consistent direction throughout the block. Templates are usually marked with a *grain line*, and this line should always be parallel to the direction of the threads when marking fabric with patchwork shapes.

Piecing The basic process of patchwork, involving a patch of one fabric being joined to a patch of another fabric by means of a narrow seam. This seam can be done by hand or machine.

Piecing order Refers to the order in which the patches are joined together. A particular piecing order is suggested for all the pieced blocks in this book, and this order has been designed as the quickest and easiest way to assemble the block.

Quilting The joining of three layers together by stitching. The three layers comprise a top layer—which can be plain fabric, or pieced or appliqued patchwork—a middle layer of batting or padding, and a third layer of a backing fabric. These layers are like a sandwich, and the quilting holds all three layers together. The quilting can be done by hand, using a running stitch, or can be done on a machine.

Strip quilting A process in which strips of fabric are pieced, backed and machine-quilted in one operation. It is a very quick technique for making patchwork, with numberless possibilities for creative use of fabrics.

Template The shapes made to transfer patchwork designs onto fabric and prepare the fabric for piecing. Templates can also be made to mark repetitive quilting designs. They are usually made from firm cardboard, but plastic sheets specially made for this purpose are also available.

1

Materials and equipment

One of the most appealing aspects of patchwork as a craft is that its materials and equipment consist of things that you already have or can easily obtain. Your nearest fabric shop, haberdasher, and stationer should be able to supply you with most of the necessities. However, there is an increasing number of specialist shops around, so do consult the list of suppliers at the end of this book. Most of these suppliers welcome mail orders from people without ready access to shops.

Fabric

Fabrics for piecing and appliqué

Cotton fabrics with a firm fine weave are by far the easiest fabrics to work with, especially for applique. However, polypoplin, homespun, calico and lawn are also suitable. Generally, I choose a fabric because of its colour or print, rather than its fibre content. Other fabrics, such as silk, can be used but they are much more difficult to sew, and I would not recommend them for beginners. All fabrics should be prewashed and pressed before using, especially if the item you are making will be washed later. It is disastrous for a colour to run or a fabric to shrink after you have finished a masterpiece—better to make sure before you begin! Unbleached calico, especially, needs prewashing to remove all the sizing in the fabric. It may need to be washed several times.

Fabrics for backing

Give careful thought to the fabric you are going to use on the back of your patchwork. For hand quilting, I suggest using any soft fabric that is not too tightly woven. I like to use a good quality, soft lawn in a plain colour which will show up all the quilting patterns. A print fabric tends to hide the quilting, but you may choose to use a print for precisely this reason (if you change colours of quilting threads, or if you are machine quilting). While sheeting can be suitable, check to see

that it is not too tightly woven and therefore difficult to quilt. Unbleached calico is unsuitable as a backing for hand quilting, as it is unpleasant to stitch through. However, for machine quilting, a firmer fabric is suitable, so it is possible to use unbleached calico. A print can look most attractive and will hide any starts and stops you make.

Batting

Polyester batting is readily available, and comes in different widths and thicknesses. A thicker batting will give your work greater puffiness when it is quilted, but it will be much harder to stitch by hand or machine because of its extra bulk. A thinner, firmer batting is generally used for strip quilting.

Threads

Threads for piecing and appliqué

Any of the widely available threads used for dressmaking are suitable for use in patchwork. They come in a wide range of colours, which is especially important for applique, where you will want to match the colour of the thread to the applique pieces. In machine piecing, it is generally acceptable to use a white thread throughout, as often you will be joining a light and a dark patch together, and the stitching will be hidden in the seam anyway. If you are hand piecing (particularly if you are sewing dark-coloured patches) you may wish to match the colour of the thread to the dark fabric.

Quilting threads

For hand quilting you will need to buy thread specially made for this purpose. Quilting requires strong thread, because ordinary threads fray and quickly wear through as you sew. Quilting threads are widely available now, and can be found in various colours. Generally, it is not important to match the colour of the quilting thread to the patchwork, because you will find that the quilting stitches form a broken line, and will tend to blend into whatever colour fabric you are quilting. Sometimes, however, you may wish to match the thread for a special effect—always do what you think is right for each individual item. The only really satisfactory substitute I have found for quilting thread is very fine crochet thread.

For machine quilting, any of the threads suitable for machine sewing can be used. As machine quilting forms a continuous line it is more obtrusive than hand quilting. Therefore it is generally desirable to match the colour of the thread to the patchwork, changing colour as necessary. Nylon invisible thread can be used, and this will blend into all colours. The invisible thread should be used as the top thread of the machine only, and not in the bobbin. In all machine quilting and strip quilting, match the bobbin thread to the colour of your backing fabric.

Tracing paper

Tracing paper is needed to copy designs from books and to make patterns for applique.

Cardboard

Firm cardboard is needed to make template shapes for piecing. Plastic sheets are now available that can be substituted for this, and the plastic will wear longer than cardboard. However, I usually use cardboard because it is easy to obtain.

Graph paper

Graph paper is used to help in making templates for simple geometric shapes. Large sheets can also be used to help with enlarging the applique designs from this book. Because graph paper comes conveniently marked with measurements, it speeds up the process of making templates and drawing designs.

Sewing machine

The largest and most important piece of equipment used in patchwork is the sewing machine. Not that patchwork must be done by machine (see 'Piecing', p. 10), but for speed,

strength (and of course machine quilting) a machine is essential. The machine does not need to be capable of anything fancy to be suitable. For piecing and quilting, it only has to do straight stitching. However, for machine quilting, you may need to experiment to find out which particular foot works best. On some machines this will be the regular foot, but on others the zipper or roller foot works best. Some machines have a dual feed which helps the three layers to move smoothly through the machine, and this feature is especially good for machine quilting. Consult the supplier of your brand of machine for advice on what is most suitable for you.

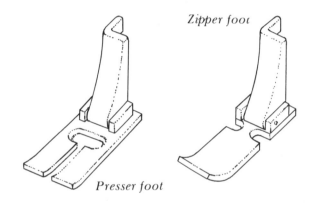

Zipper foot

Presser foot

Iron

An iron will constantly be needed when you are piecing, to press the patchwork as you put it together. This ensures a smooth neat finish to the surface, with all the seams lying flat on the wrong side. I emphasise 'pressing' rather than 'ironing', as the latter suggests too vigorous an approach which might stretch or distort your work. While patchwork is pressed continuously as it is being made, quilting should not be pressed at all, because the iron fuses and flattens the batting.

Scissors

Sharp scissors, that easily cut fabric, make a big difference when you are cutting several hundred patches for a quilt. Try to keep your fabric-cutting scissors exclusively for that purpose, and use another pair for cutting paper and cardboard. A pair of thread snippers are very useful to have by the machine when you are piecing, to snip off all the ends as you go—this is a boring job to do later!

Rotary cutter and mat

A rotary cutter is a very sharp circular blade on a handle, and is particularly useful for cutting strips of fabric. The cutter needs to be used with a special mat, which can be purchased along with it.

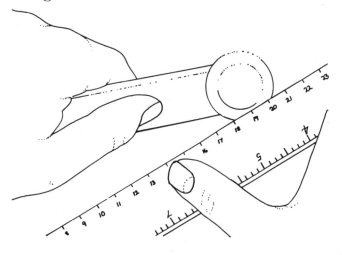

Pins

Pins are constantly used in patchwork for a variety of purposes, from pinning small patches together to pinning whole quilts together ready for machine quilting. I like to use pins with glass heads, as they are slightly longer than ordinary pins (and also much easier to spot when they inevitably fall on the floor!).

Needles

For appliqué and piecing by hand, you can use any kind of needle that you find comfortable and easy to use. For tacking (basting) a quilt ready for hand quilting, you will need a long needle. However, quilting requires special needles called *betweens*, which are very short. These needles are available at haberdashery shops or departments, and come in a packet containing a range of sizes.

Thimbles

A thimble really is essential when quilting, to push the needle through the three layers being quilted. Even if you have never used a thimble before, persist with it when you are learning to quilt. You will soon find it becomes comfortable, and you may begin to use it for all your hand sewing. Choose a thimble which fits your finger without being too tight, yet does not drop off easily. I like to use two thimbles when I quilt. One, as is usual, on the middle finger of the hand that holds the needle, but also one on the pointer finger of the hand under the quilting. The quilting action involves just grazing the finger with the tip of the needle, and this second thimble protects your finger.

Quilting hoop

One of the few special pieces of equipment for quilting is a hoop to hold the three layers evenly while you quilt. Hoops come in a variety of sizes, and should be chosen to suit the length of your arm because at any one time you can only quilt as far as the distance between your fingers and elbow. A hoop 45 cm (18″) in diameter is the size most people find comfortable.

Quilting frames

It is possible to obtain small, square frames that can be used to quilt cushions and other small pieces. However, most people generally prefer to quilt these on their laps without a frame, or else enlarge the backing fabric so they can quilt on a hoop. Full-sized quilting frames are really only necessary if you want several people to work on a quilt at one time. While elaborate frames can be made, a perfectly satisfactory one can be simply constructed from two long pieces of wood with strips of fabric stapled to them, and two shorter pieces of wood which act as stretchers. If holes are drilled at the ends of the long pieces, and at regular intervals along the shorter pieces, the frame can be bolted together with bolts and wing nuts.

Pencils

You will need good sharp pencils with which to draw your templates, and to mark your fabrics. You need a white or yellow coloured pencil to mark dark fabrics and, if you have a block with reverse shapes, you might find it convenient to mark the shapes in one colour (red for example) then mark the reverse shapes in another colour (such as blue) so that you do not confuse the two.

Rulers

A ruler is necessary for drawing and measuring your template shapes. There are also special patchwork rulers available that are particularly useful in measuring and cutting strips. These transparent plastic rulers are wide, and have divisions marked across their entire width so that you can lay the ruler directly on the fabric to measure it. Another useful special ruler that is available is a narrow one that marks just the width of the 6 mm (¼″) seam allowance used in piecing.

Glue

You will need glue or a glue stick to glue the template shapes onto cardboard once you have cut them from paper or graph paper.

Masking tape

Masking tape is very useful for marking lines ready for quilting. The tape is laid on the top of the quilt, and you quilt along outside it. It provides a quick way for making straight lines without a lot of tedious marking, and the tape can be used and reused many times. It can even be used around curves if it is snipped along one side.

Using colour in patchwork

Colour is *the* most important ingredient in successful patchwork. A piece of patchwork in attractive colours will always be much admired, even if it is less than perfect in technique. However, another piece which may be perfect in every detail, with accurate piecing and fine stitching, is less appealing if the colour combinations are unimaginative.

It is impossible to completely cover such a large subject in a book like this and, because an awareness of basic colour theory is an advantage in patchwork, you might like to look for a good book on colour theory that you can either borrow or buy. Nevertheless, I would like to make a few suggestions which you may find useful:

- Ultimately, choice of colour is completely personal and subjective. There are no rights or wrongs, only combinations which work and (beyond that) combinations which please you, the creator. Different colours appeal to different people, so use your patchwork to express *your* colour preferences.

- Tone is a very important ingredient in successful colour choices for patchwork. By tone I mean how dark or how light a colour is. For instance, pale blue is a light tone, and purple is a dark tone. Patchwork should contain a variety of tones. If you want a strong contrast, use colours from both ends of the tonal scale. For example, a deep blue could be used against a light caramel. For a softer, more subtle effect, use colours that are closer together on the tonal scale, e.g. pale pink and apple green. Check the tonal values in your patchwork by looking at it with your eyes half-closed.

- An entire quilt can be planned around a fabric print that you fall in love with, and this is often a very useful way of working. Look for a print that you like, analyse the colours in it, then select other colours which develop the print.

- Don't be too set in your ideas. It is possible to plan a wonderful blue quilt on paper and then, when you go shopping, find that the colours you want are just not available this season.

- Play with the colours available—arrange them in a sequence . . . change them round . . . try different ones, till you come up with a combination you like.

- Don't play it too safe. While monotone colour schemes (that is, colour schemes based on one colour) always work, there is always the danger of them looking dull and uninteresting.

- Keep looking at your work from a distance. Colours change and interact in unexpected ways that you may not be aware of when working up close.

- When you find yourself confused, put away your work, even if only for a short time. Then bring it out again, and look at it with 'fresh eyes'. Often this will help you spot the problem immediately.

- Patchwork is generally improved if you have a variety in the types of print that you use. Try to avoid an item having all 'busy', little prints by also using some larger prints if possible.

- Nature is the best guide to colour. When you next admire a sunset, a leaf, or a flower, look at it more closely. Ask yourself exactly what colours are in it. You may find some surprises.

Facing: **Ashes of Roses** *quilt made by Judy Turner. Showing subtle gradations of tonal values and skilful blending of colour, this quilt was all made from one simple triangle shape. It was machine pieced and hand quilted.*

Developing a sense of colour

Here are some colour exercises you might like to try, using old coloured magazines, scissors and glue:

- Enlarge and copy the colour wheel below. Cut out bits of coloured magazines and glue appropriate colours in the spaces.

- Make a tonal scale by cutting out bits of paper in one colour and arranging them from light to dark. Try to make the scale extend from nearly white through to nearly black. Keep checking the tonal values by looking through half-closed eyes.

- Find a natural object such as a rock, leaf or piece of bark. Analyse the colours in it, then cut out pieces of paper that match all these colours in their correct proportions of size and occurance.

- Investigate a single colour. For instance, cut out as many different shades of red as you can find, and stick them onto a piece of paper so that no background shows through.

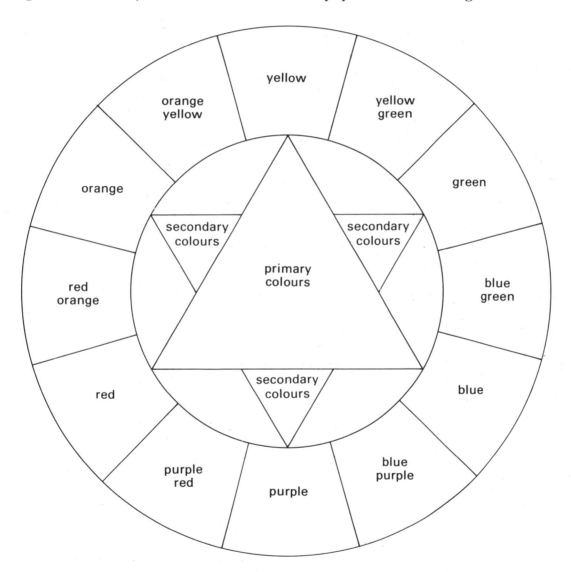

Facing: **Brolgas at Thylungra** *wallhanging by Wendy Saclier. With colours evocative of the Australian outback, Wendy has portrayed a memory from her childhood. Annually the brolgas danced on the claypan, with grey-green gidgee and mulga trees behind, and brick-orange sandhills in the distance beneath a cloudless sky. The wallhanging was machine pieced and hand quilted, with details hand embroidered.*

Making templates

The basis of accurate patchwork is to start with accurate templates. It is worth taking time and trouble to prepare your templates carefully, as it is very frustrating to reach the sewing stage and find that your original shape was not correct. I usually make templates out of firm cardboard, but it is also possible to buy special plastic for making them.

There are two different types of templates, those *without* a seam allowance added, and those *with* a seam allowance.

Templates without a seam allowance

These templates are shapes that are the exact size of the finished patch, without any seams allowed for. If using simple shapes such as squares, triangles and rectangles (or if you are devising your own blocks) I recommend making the template shapes from graph paper first, as graph paper comes already marked into convenient divisions, with accurate measurements and exact right angles. You can also use graph paper to help you when altering the *size* of templates to make them suit the size of your project.

For more involved template shapes, such as the ones in this book, you need to trace or copy the shapes very accurately. (Note: all the template shapes in this book are *without seam allowances*.)

When you draw around a template shape on the wrong side of the fabric, the line you draw becomes your *sewing* line. You need to cut out the fabric 6 mm (¼″) outside these lines to provide the seam allowances.

Templates without seam allowance are usually used for piecing by hand, as you can follow the pencilled seam line with your stitching. I also prefer to use these templates for piecing more complex blocks on the machine, so that angles and small pieces are exact.

Some people prefer to make templates without seam allowances, and then mark the exact seam allowance on the fabric as well. A special narrow ruler, the size of the seam allowance, is useful for doing this. It is important to mark an exact seam allowance when you are doing curved seams.

Using graph paper to make templates without seam allowances

Step 1
Draw your template shape on graph paper, using a sharp pencil and ruler.

Step 2
Cut out the template shape, and glue it to a piece of cardboard.

Step 3
Cut out the cardboard exactly along the edges of the graph paper. Label the shape, and then mark the grain line on the reverse side if necessary.

Copying templates

Step 1
Place tracing paper over the page of shapes, and use paper clips to secure the tracing paper in place.

Step 2
Draw the shapes carefully by marking each corner or joint with a dot. Then use a ruler to join the dots. Keep comparing your traced shape with the original to see that the tracing paper has not moved or that no distortion has occurred. If the shape has a curve, mark a series of dots along the curve, then join the dots with a smooth line. Some template shapes in this book are larger than the size of the pages, so they have been divided into parts, with the division being indicated by a broken line. Copy both parts.

Step 3
Label each template shape with the name of the block, its number, the grain line, and any notches that are marked.

Step 4
Cut out the tracing paper shape, and glue it smoothly onto firm cardboard. For shapes that are in two parts, cut out both parts, then exactly align the pieces along the broken lines so that they form one whole template shape.

Step 5
Cut around the tracing paper shape.

Step 6
If necessary, label the reverse side of each shape with its reverse number (for example, 4R) and also mark the grain line. If the grain line is not parallel with one of the edges of the reverse shape, the easiest way to mark it is to push a pin through the template at the points of the double-headed arrow marking the grain line on the tracing paper side. Turn the template over, and draw a line joining the pin marks.

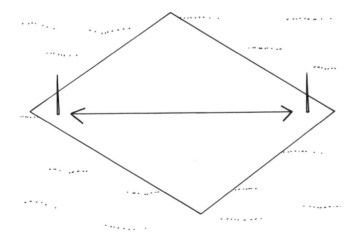

Templates with a seam allowance

These templates are shapes the size of the finished patch with an added 6 mm (¼″) all around to allow for the seams. When you draw onto the fabric, the pencil line becomes your *cutting line*, and no sewing line is marked.

These templates are particularly suitable for machine piecing, as you use the cut edges of the fabric to guide your patches through the machine, thus eliminating much pinning. I use this kind of template when I am sewing simple geometric shapes, such as squares, triangles and rectangles. I find it less satisfactory for asymmetrical shapes, or for shapes with acute angles.

While I recommend a seam allowance of 6 mm (¼″), you may wish to make it the width of your machine presser foot instead. This makes piecing very easy, as you just line up the edge of the presser foot with the cut edge of the patches. First, measure the distance between the needle and the right-hand edge of the presser foot, and this distance can then become the amount you add for the seams when making your templates.

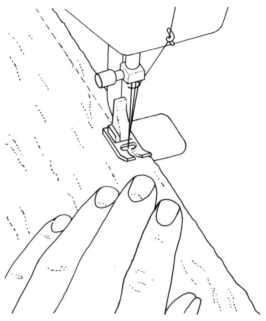

Making templates with a seam allowance

Step 1
Draw the template shape (as described earlier for making templates without a seam allowance) by either drawing them on graph paper, or copying them from the book. Label with name, number and grain line.

Step 2
Cut out the shape and glue it to cardboard.

Step 3
Draw a line 6 mm (¼″) all around the shape, making sure that the line you draw is parallel to the edge of the original shape, and that it is a constant distance of 6 mm (¼″) from the cut paper shape.

Step 4
Cut out the cardboard shape along the line you have drawn. Mark the reverse side with its number and grain line if necessary.

Piecing

Whether you wish to do your patchwork by hand or machine is a completely personal decision. Either way is right—the decision is entirely yours. Machine piecing is quick and strong, but involves solitary work at your machine. Piecing by hand takes longer and is not quite as strong as machine piecing, but it is completely portable and very pleasant to do in company.

How to do hand piecing

Hand piecing is done with a simple running stitch. Begin with a knot, and add a back stitch as well to avoid having the knot come through to the front of the work later. Finish the line of stitching with a couple of back stitches. Keep your stitches as neat and even as possible, stitching only along your seam line and not into the seam allowance. It is a good idea to match the colour of the thread to the darker of the patches that you are piecing.

Hand piecing is generally done using templates *without* seam allowances, so in this case you follow the marked line with your stitching.

How to do machine piecing

Machine piecing is like sewing seams in dressmaking, except that the seam is a narrow one of 6 mm (¼″). Set the machine on a fairly short stitch length—but not too short, in case some unpicking is necessary. Generally, straight seams are stitched right along the patches, going across the seam allowance at the beginning and end, without needing back stitches. If you need to *set-in* pieces (in situations where straight seams are not possible) you do not stitch across the seam allowances, and you will need some back stitches at the seam junction.

Machine piecing can be done using templates *without* seam allowances, in which case you follow the marked lines as for hand piecing. It also can be done using templates *with* seam allowances, in which case you use the edge of the fabric as a guide for making the correct seam width.

Piecing simple shapes

Beautiful patchwork can be made from the simplest of geometric shapes—for instance Judy Turner's quilt, **Ashes of Roses** (facing p. 6), was all made from triangles. However, if you are a beginner, it is a good idea to begin with a small project, such as a pot holder or cushion (pillow), to learn the basic techniques. But from that stage on the possibilities are endless. Simple shapes are particularly suitable for machine piecing.

Machine piecing simple shapes

Step 1
Make a template of a square, rectangle or triangle, following the instructions for making templates *with* seam allowances. The size of your template will be determined by your overall design and the planned item.

Step 2
Use the template to mark the wrong side of your fabric. On light coloured fabric use an ordinary lead pencil, and on dark coloured fabric use a white or yellow pencil. Make sure your pencils are kept very sharp, and that you mark as closely as possible to the template. It is surprising how much error can occur with a blunt pencil, or a pencil held on an angle away from the template. Make sure the grain of the fabric is in the correct direction by aligning the grain line marked on the template with the grain of the fabric.

Step 3
Cut out the fabric along the pencilled lines.

Step 4
Plan the order in which you are going to piece the patches. If you are piecing squares or

rectangles, these should first be joined together into rows, and then the rows are joined together. If you are joining right-angled triangles, then these should first be joined into squares, the squares into rows, and then the rows joined together. It should always be possible to sew straight seams.

Step 5
Begin sewing the patches together in the order planned in Step 4. When sewing the patches together, it should not be necessary to pin them until you get to the stage of having to match seams. Just lay one patch on top of another, right sides together, and feed them through the machine, making a 6 mm (¼″) seam. Stitch right along from one edge of the fabric to the other, stitching across the seam allowance. You do not need to begin and end with a back stitch. If you are sewing multiples of the same shapes, you can feed them through the machine in a chain.

Step 6
Press all the seams to one side. The finish of the completed patchwork depends very much on conscientious pressing at each stage. When sewing your patches into rows, press all the seams of any one row in the same direction, but alternate this direction from every row to the next.

Step 7
When you have finished piecing the rows, and they are all pressed, they can be pinned together. It is important to pin at this stage, so that the seams match exactly. Pressing the seams in different directions (as suggested in Step 6) helps the seams to sit flat. Put your pins in at right angles to the seam you are about to stitch, easing any fullness by putting in more pins if necessary.

Step 8
Stitch the rows together, being sure to stitch very carefully over the pins. (You may prefer to pull them out as you come to them.)

Step 9
Press the finished patchwork well.

Hand piecing simple shapes

Follow the directions given for machine piecing, except make the templates *without* a seam allowance. This means that the line you

mark becomes your *sewing* line, rather than your cutting line, and you must add a seam allowance beyond this line when you cut out your pieces. The pieces will also need pinning together to correctly align the sewing lines before you begin to sew.

Piecing block designs

All the pieced block designs in this book measure 30 cm (12″) square when finished. Some of the designs are suitable for alteration of the block size (see below in *'Changing the size of the blocks'*).

Reverse shapes

Many of the blocks include reverse shapes which are shapes labelled with a number followed by the letter R. For example, the reverse shape for piece 3 would be labelled 3R. These reverse shapes are the mirror images of the corresponding template shapes, and therefore are *not interchangeable* with the original shapes. The reverse shapes are made by turning the template over when marking the fabric. For asymmetrical blocks, such as **Kangaroo paw** or **Pink heath**, it is important that the templates be face down as you mark (otherwise the whole block will emerge as a mirror image of the original). This means reverse shapes will actually be face *up* as you mark. For symmetrical blocks this is not so important, and you can mark the shapes face up if you wish, with just the reverse shapes face down.

When marking reverse shapes, it may be helpful to use a different coloured pencil, to distinguish between the pieces. For instance, you could use a red pencil for shapes and a blue pencil for reverse shapes.

Piecing a block design

Step 1
Copy the templates for the block you want (as already described in *'Making templates without a seam allowance'*). Note that all the template shapes in this book *do not* include a seam allowance.

Step 2
Use the templates to mark the fabric by placing them on the wrong side of the fabric.

For the symmetrical blocks, the templates can be face up and the reverse shapes face down. However, as already pointed out, with asymmetrical blocks the templates must be face down as you mark, which means that the reverse shapes will actually be face up as you mark.

When marking, be careful to match the grain of the fabric with the grain line indicated on the template by the double-headed arrow. Mark any notches.

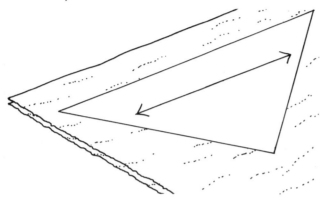

Remember to leave 6 mm (¼″) around each piece for a seam allowance—that is, leave 12 mm (½″) between any two pieces.

Refer back to the original diagram to work out the number of pieces to cut out for each block.

Step 3

Cut out all the marked shapes, 6 mm (¼″) from the marked lines. Remember, *do not cut along the marked lines*, as these are the stitching lines.

Step 4

Lay out the pieces of the block on a table or board, referring to the diagram for the correct placement of the pieces. This is an important step to prevent you making mistakes when you are sewing the pieces together. As any pieces are sewn together, always replace them correctly in the laid out design.

Step 5

Follow the piecing order set out for each block, as this order has been designed to make the piecing as simple as possible. The symbol '+' means to join, and when the pieces are joined, the units they make are put in brackets. For example, if pieces 1 and 2 must be joined first, and then piece 3 added to the unit made by 1 and 2, the instructions look like this:

1   1 + 2
2   (1,2) + 3

- If piece 4 is the next added, the instructions will be like this:

  3   (1,2,3) + 4

- If, after that, pieces 5 and 6 need to be joined together before they are added, the instructions will continue:

  4   5 + 6
  5   (1,2,3,4) + (5,6)

- If pieces need to be added to both sides of a piece or unit, the instructions will look like this:

  6   7 + (1,2,3,4,5,6) + 8

Step 6

Pin pieces together by putting pins into the corners first, exactly into the corners you have marked, then pinning the rest of the seam.

Step 7

Sew along the lines marked on the fabric. The piecing order has been designed so that, wherever possible, all seams are straight seams —which may be sewn by hand, or by machine from one edge of the fabric to the other (with the machine stitching going across the seam allowance). The exception to this is when the instructions tell you to *set-in* a piece (see 'Set-in piecing' below).

Step 8

Press all the seams after sewing, pressing the seam allowances to one side unless the instructions indicate otherwise.

Set-in piecing

Where straight seams have not been possible, the piecing order will tell you to *set-in* a piece. This occurs when there is a Y-shaped junction of three seams, and it is done by seaming exactly along the marked lines, and not sewing into the seam allowance. The seams should be sewn in three steps, realigning the seams before each step. When sewing on a machine, the stitching at the point of the 'Y' junction should be secured with a couple of back stitches.

Curved piecing

Two of the block designs, **Gum Blossom** and **Sydney Opera House**, involve piecing together curved shapes. This should not be difficult as long as a few precautions are taken in the marking, cutting and pinning stages.

You will notice that all the templates of the curved pieces have been marked with notches. On your templates, snip the centre out of these notches and mark the notches on the seam line when you are marking the fabric. The notches are marked on both of the curved pieces to be joined, and should be aligned when you are pinning the pieces together.

When cutting out the curved pieces, make sure you cut an exact 6 mm (¼″) seam allowance along the curved edges, as this makes lining up and sewing the pieces together very much easier. It is a good idea to specially mark the 6 mm (¼″) seam allowance on these pieces before you cut them out.

Pin the curved pieces together very carefully. First pin the ends, then pin at each notch, encroaching ever so slightly into the seam allowance with the pin. As you sew, keep the two cut edges together, and the two pieces should just fit together as you make the seam. I generally find it unnecessary to clip into the seam allowance, since the material in the seam allowance should ease into place.

Press the seam allowance to the concave (inward curving) side.

Changing the size of blocks

Some block designs can be easily made larger, or made smaller to be used in designs for clothing, for example. Examples of this can be seen in the garments made by Linda McGuire using **Banksia** and **Cooktown orchid** blocks. These blocks, illustrated below, have been designed using geometric divisions of a square. The divisions are indicated by the dotted lines. To alter the size of the blocks, draw a square the size you want (graph paper will help to do this) mark it into the same divisions indicated by the dotted lines, then draw the block design. The shapes can then be copied to make your templates.

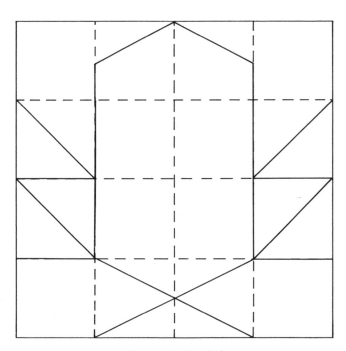

Figure A: **Banksia**

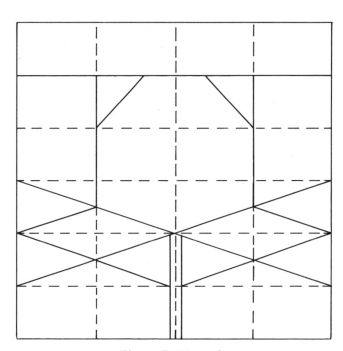

Figure B: **Waratah**

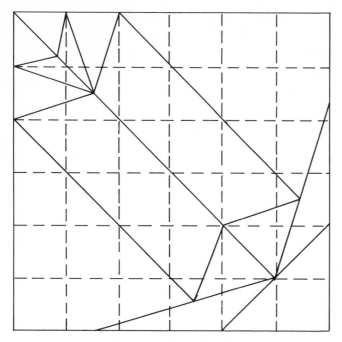

Figure C: **Bottlebrush**

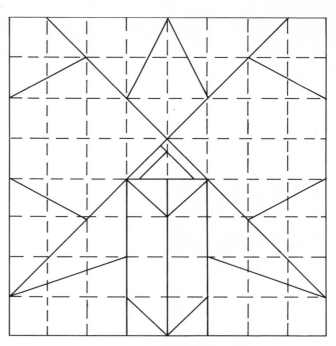

Figure D: **Cooktown orchid**

Facing: **Gumnut Babies** *cot quilt by Anne Moten. Squares from furnishing fabric printed with the popular gumnut babies design were used to make a simple cot quilt which was machine pieced and both machine and hand quilted.*

Following page: Potholders and strip-quilted place mats made by Judy Turner. These attractive and practical items have been made using simple piecing and strip quilting. They are enhanced by fabric printed with Australian motifs. Directions for potholders (p. 133), and placemats (p. 138).

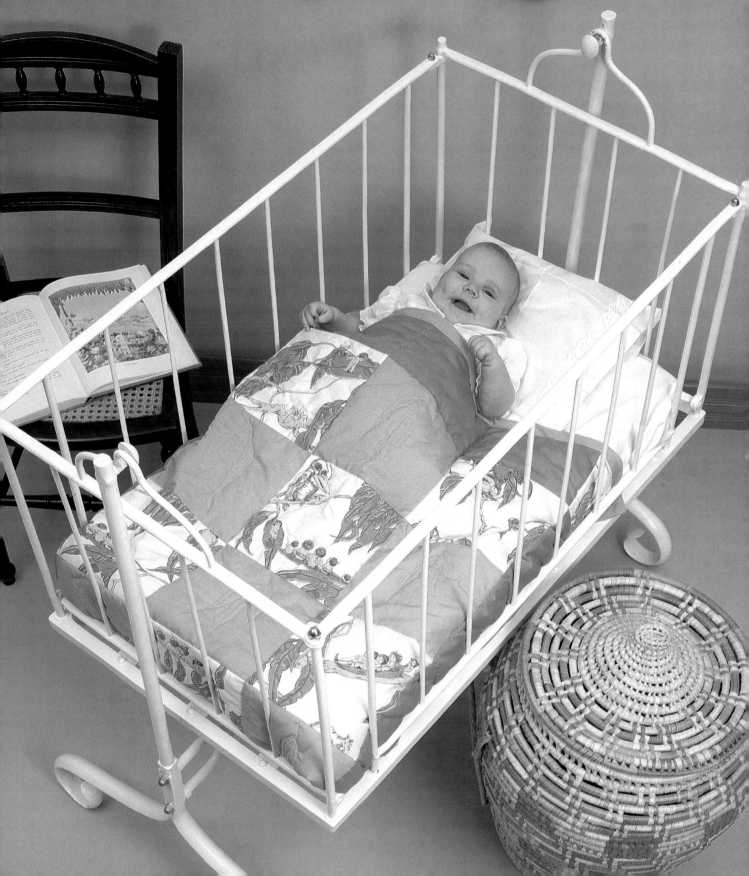

Step-by-step: Piecing simple shapes

Step 1 Using a template *with* seam allowances added, mark fabric on wrong side with a sharp pencil. This line becomes your *cutting line*.

Step 2 Cut out the shapes, along the marked pencil lines.

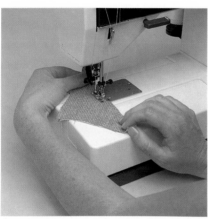

Step 3 Without pinning, put pieces right sides together and feed through machine. Stitch from one cut edge to the other, making a 6 mm (¼″) seam.

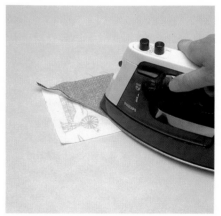

Step 4 Press seam allowances to one side. After sewing the pieces into rows, press seams of alternate rows in opposite directions.

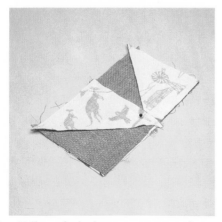

Step 5 When joining rows together, match the pieces at the already sewn seams. Pin in place, putting pins at right angles to the seam. Stitch and press.

Step 6 A finished square of simple shapes constructed into a pot holder.

Step-by-step: Piecing a block design

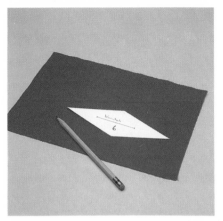

Step 1 Using a template *without* seam allowances added, mark fabric on wrong side with a sharp pencil. This lines becomes your *sewing line.*

Step 2 Cut out the shapes, cutting 6 mm (¼″) outside the marked line.

Step 3 Lay out the pieces of the block in their correct position, replacing them in position after sewing. Follow the piecing order given to sew the pieces together.

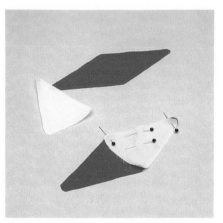

Step 4 Pin pieces together before stitching. Poke pins through at the ends of the seam line to align both seam lines. Add more pins to secure the pieces together.

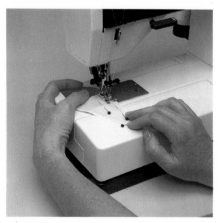

Step 5 Stitch along marked line from one cut edge to the other, unless a 'set-in' seam is required (when you only stitch on the seam line). Press seams.

Step 6 A finished **Waratah** block, from the **Floral emblems** wallhanging.

Banksia

- ▨ Orange, or yellow
- ▦ Green
- ▢ Background

Piecing order

1. 1 + 2 green
2. 1R + 2 green
3. 2 background + 2 green; repeat once.
4. (1,2) + (2,2) +3
5. (1R,2) + (2,2) +3
6. 5 + 4 +5R
7. (5,4,5R) + 6
8. 6 + 7
9. (5,4,5R,6) + (6,7)
10. (1,2,2,2,3) + (5,4,5R,6,6,7) + (1R,2,2,2,3)

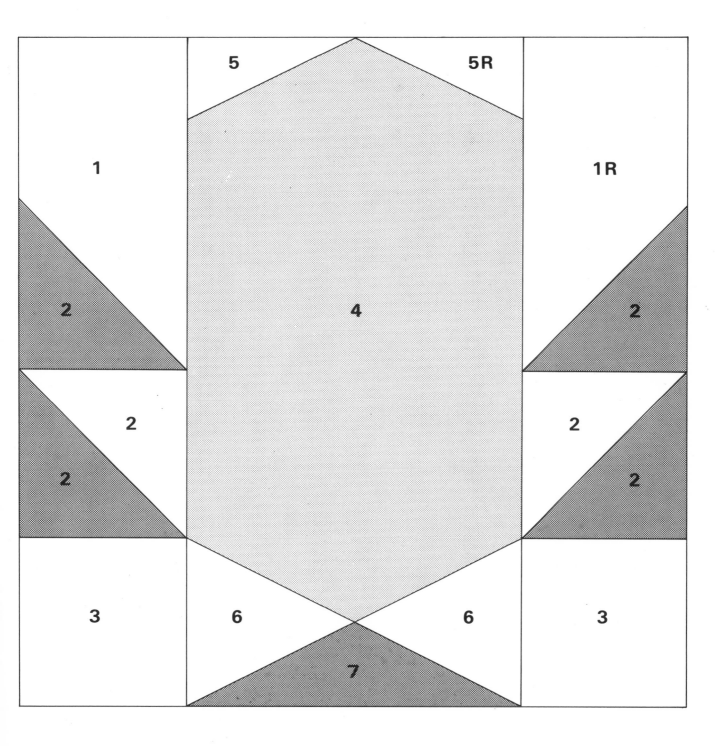

4

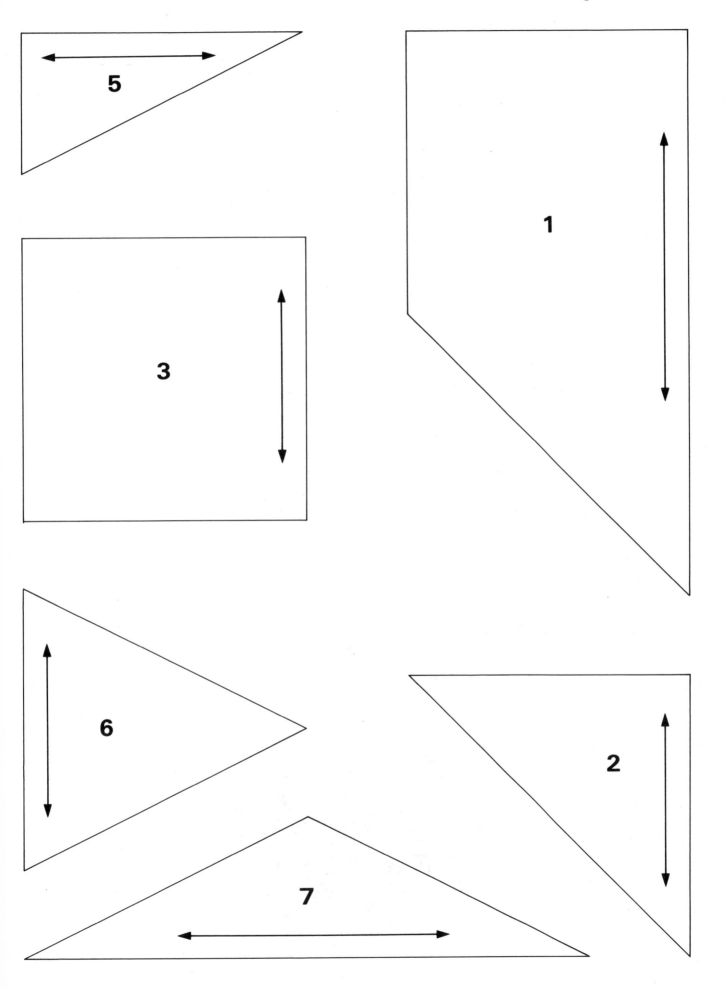

Purple flag

■ Yellow

▨ Purple

■ Green

☐ Background

Piecing order

1 1 + 2; repeat twice.

2 (1,2) + 3 + (1,2) + 3

3 4 + 5 + 6, matching notches.

4 (4,5,6) + 7

5 4R + 5R + 6R, matching notches.

6 (4R,5R,6R) + 7R

7 (4,5,6,7) + 8 + (4R,5R,6R,7R) +(1,2)

8 (4,5,6,7,8,4R,5R,6R,7R,1,2) + (1,2,3,1,2,3). Pin carefully at the centre for this step.

9 Add the four 9 pieces to the square thus formed, to complete the block.

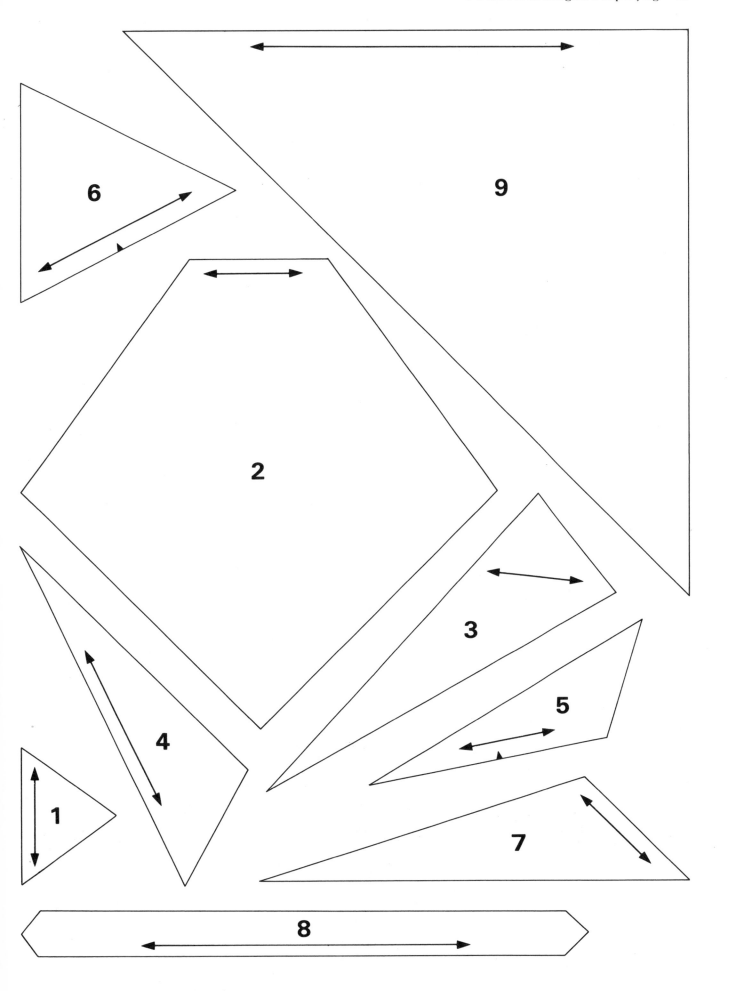

Waratah

- ▒ Red print, or red
- ▓ Red
- ■ Green
- ☐ Background

Piecing order

1 2 + 1 + 2
2 3 + (2,1,2) + 3R
3 (3,2,1,2,3R) + 4
4 5 + 6 + 5; repeat once.
5 7 + 8 + 9
6 7 + 8R + 9
7 (7,8,9) + 10 + (7,8R,9)
8 (7,8,9,10,7,8R,9) + (5,6,5)
9 (3,2,1,3R,4) + (5,6,5)
10 (7,8,9,10,7,8R,9,5,6,5) + (3,2,1,2,3R,4,5,6,5)
Pin this seam carefully.

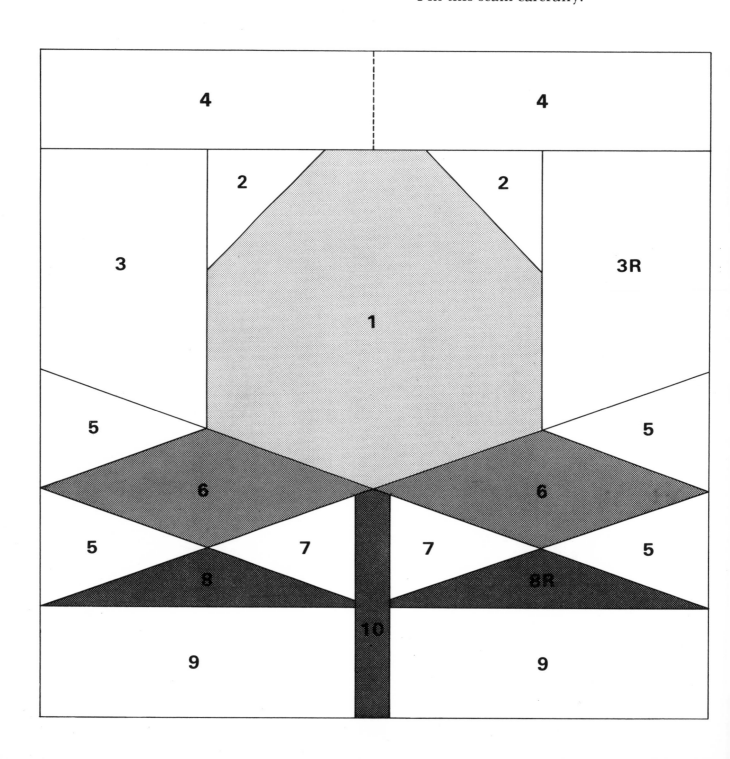

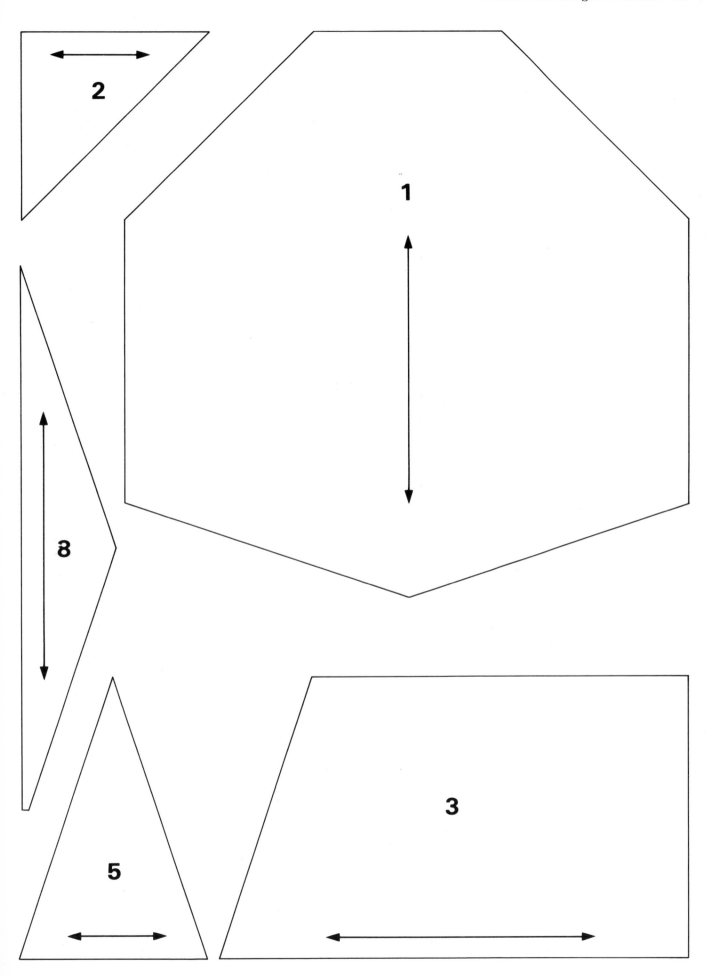

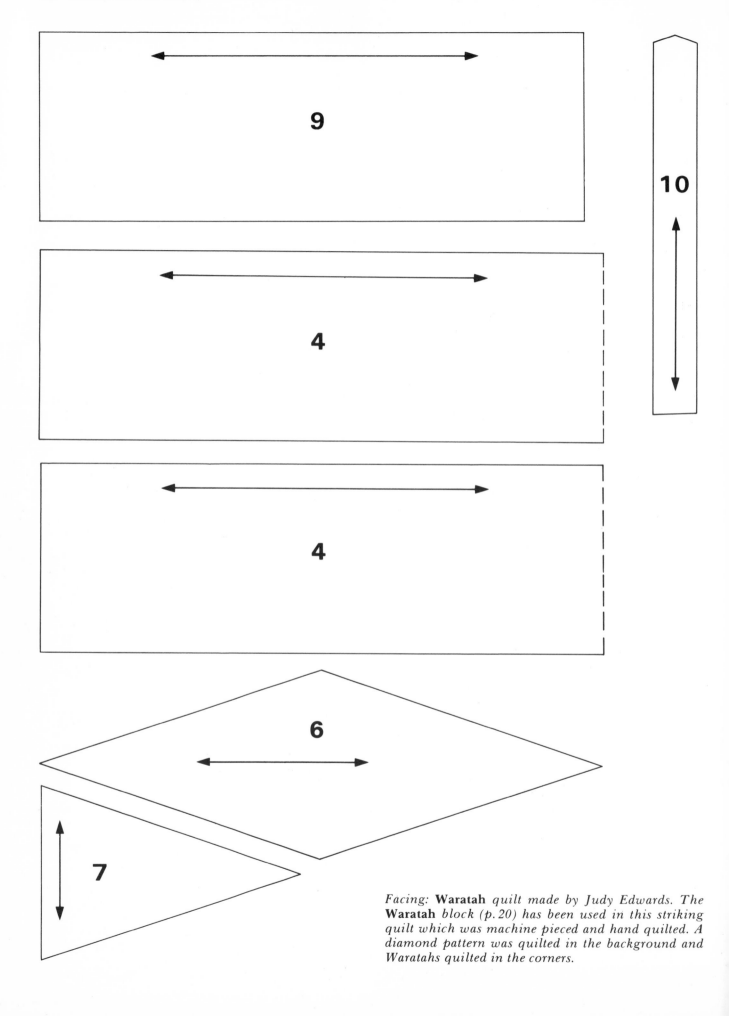

Facing: **Waratah** *quilt made by Judy Edwards. The* **Waratah** *block (p. 20) has been used in this striking quilt which was machine pieced and hand quilted. A diamond pattern was quilted in the background and Waratahs quilted in the corners.*

Sturt's desert pea

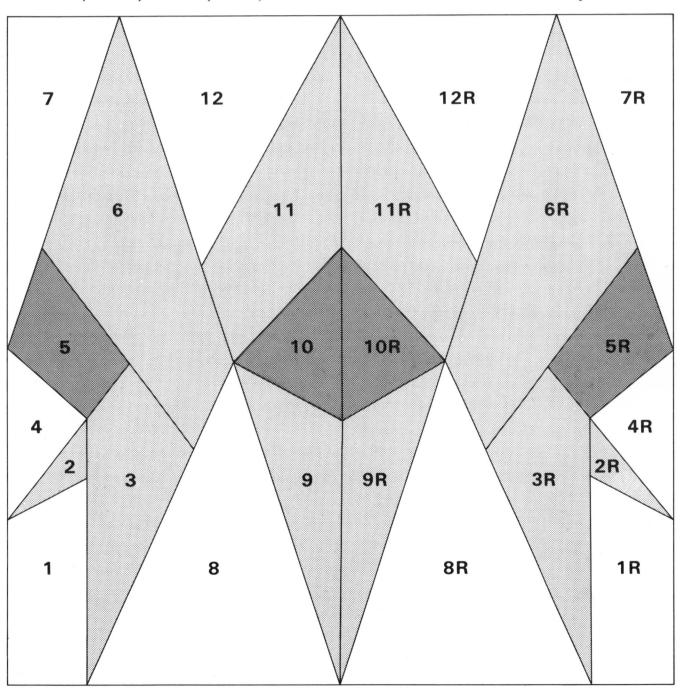

Red

Black

Background

Facing: **Sturt's desert pea** *quilt by the author. The vibrant colours of the Sturt's desert pea contrast with the cream background symbolising the desert while green diamonds, suggesting leaves, link the pieced blocks. The quilt was pieced and quilted by machine.*

Piecing order

1 1 + 2
2 (1,2) + 3
3 4 + 5
4 (1,2,3) + (4,5)
5 (1,2,3,4,5) + 6
6 7 + (1,2,3,4,5,6) + 8
7 9 + 10
8 (9,10) + 11 + 12
9 (1,2,3,4,5,6,7,8) + (9,10,11,12)
10 Repeat steps 1 to 9 using all the reverse pieces, i.e. 1R + 2R etc.
11 Join the two halves together to complete the block. Press this seam open.

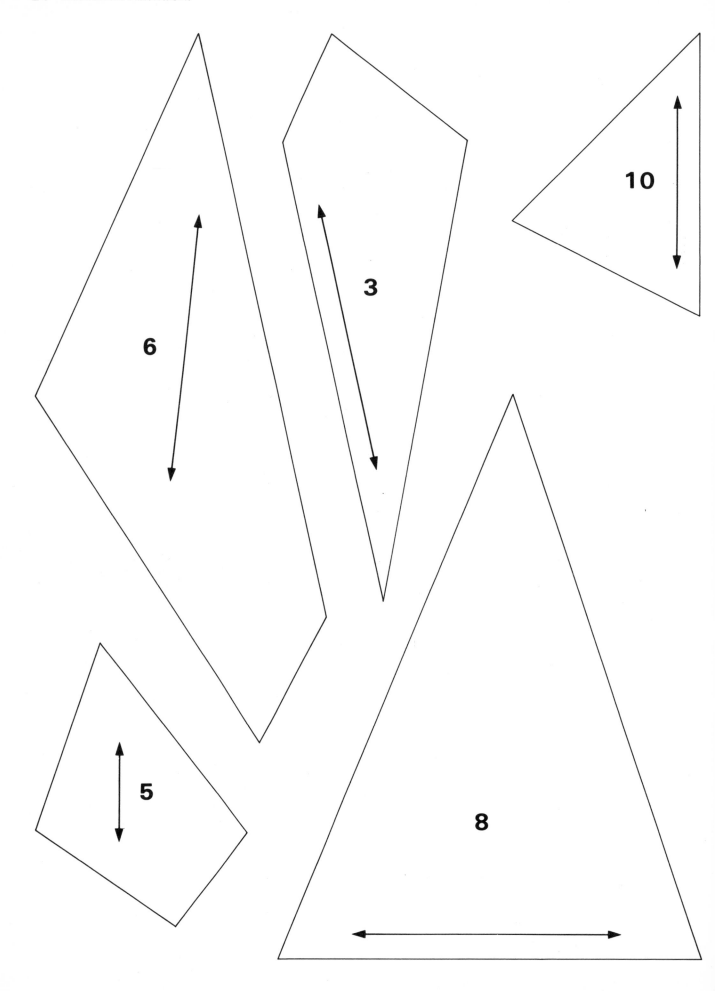

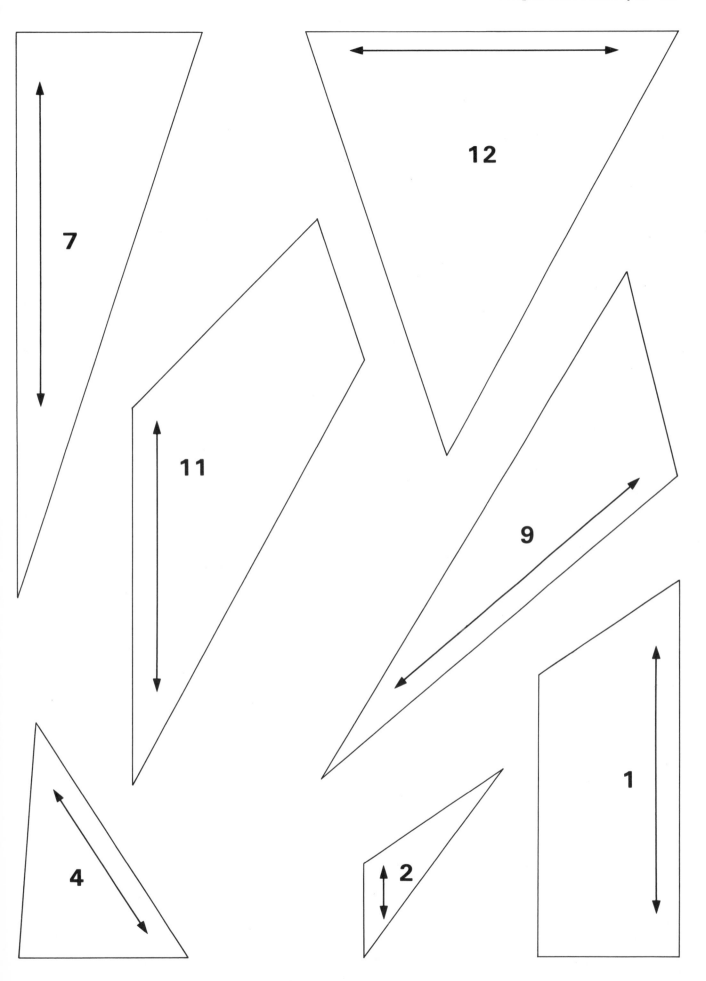

Sturt's desert rose

designed by Philip Rolfe

- ☐ Yellow
- ■ Maroon
- ☐ Pale pink
- ▨ Green
- ☐ Background

Piecing order

1 2 + 1 + 2
2 3 + (2,1,2) + 3
3 4 + 5 + 4; repeat once. Press seams towards 5.
4 5 + (3,2,1,2,3) + 5. Press seams towards 5.
5 (4,5,4) + (5,3,2,1,2,3,5) + (4,5,4)
6 6 + 7; repeat three more times. Press seams towards 6.
7 6R + 8; repeat three more times. Press seams towards 6R.
8 (6,7) + (6R,8); repeat three more times.
9 Add (6,7,6R,8) units to each side of the centre square of (4,5,4,5,3,2,1,2,3,5,4,5,4)

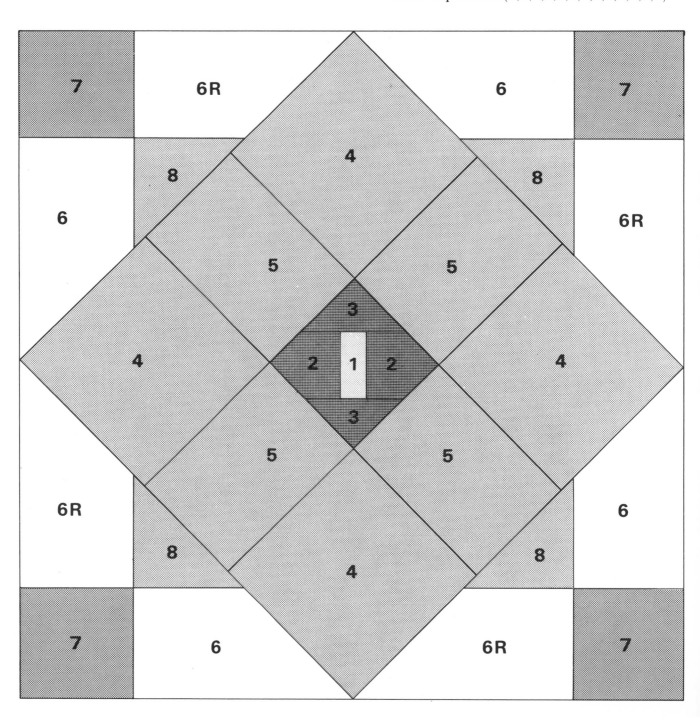

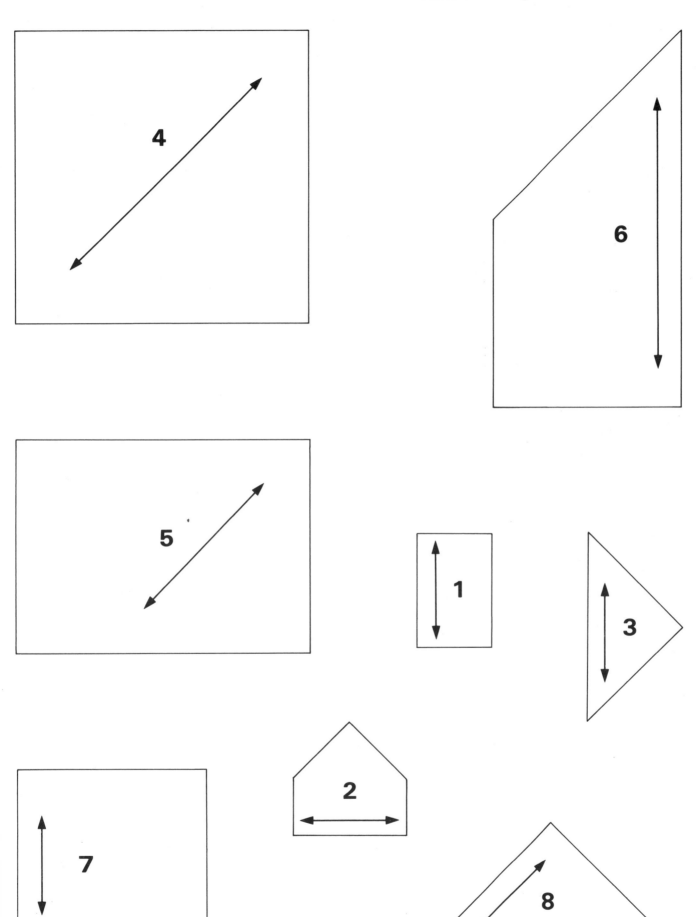

Cooktown orchid

- ☐ Pink
- ☒ Yellow
- ■ Magenta, or deep pink
- ☐ Background

Piecing order

1. 1 + 2
2. (1,2) + 3
3. 4 magenta + 5 + 4 background
4. 4R magenta + 5R + 4R background
5. (4,5,4) + (4R,5R,4R) Press this seam open.
6. (1,2,3) + (4,5,4,4R,5R,4R)
7. 6 + 7
8. 6R + 7R

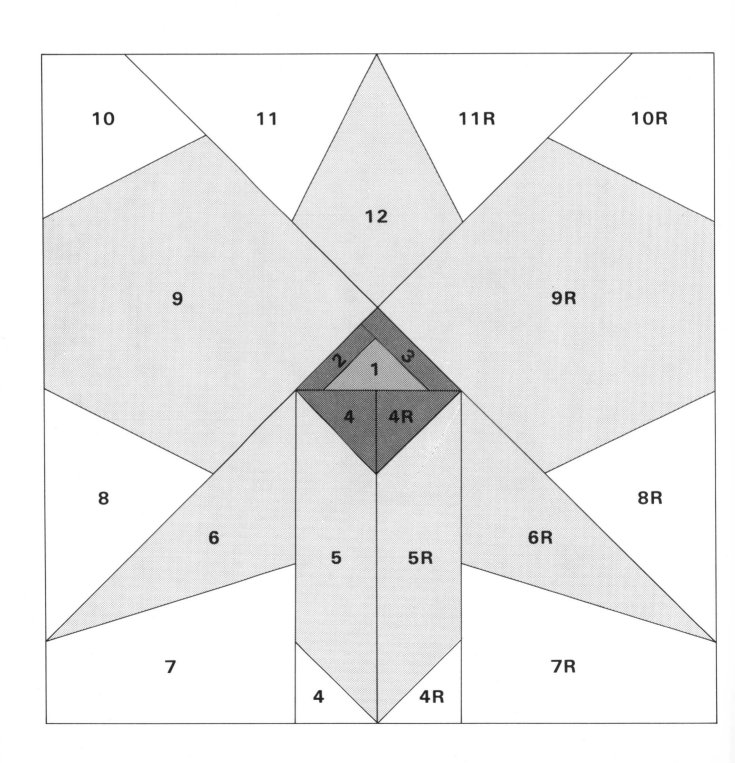

9 (6,7) + (1,2,3,4,5,4,4R,5R,4R) + (6R,7R)
10 8 + 9 + 10
11 8R + 9R + 10R
12 11 + 12 + 11R
13 (8,9,10) + (11,12,11R)
14 (6,7,1,2,3,4,5,4,4R,5R,4R,6R,7R) +
     (8R,9R,10R)
15 (6,7,1,2,3,4,5,4,4R,5R,4R,6R,7R,8R,
     9R,10R) + (8,9,10,11,12,11R)

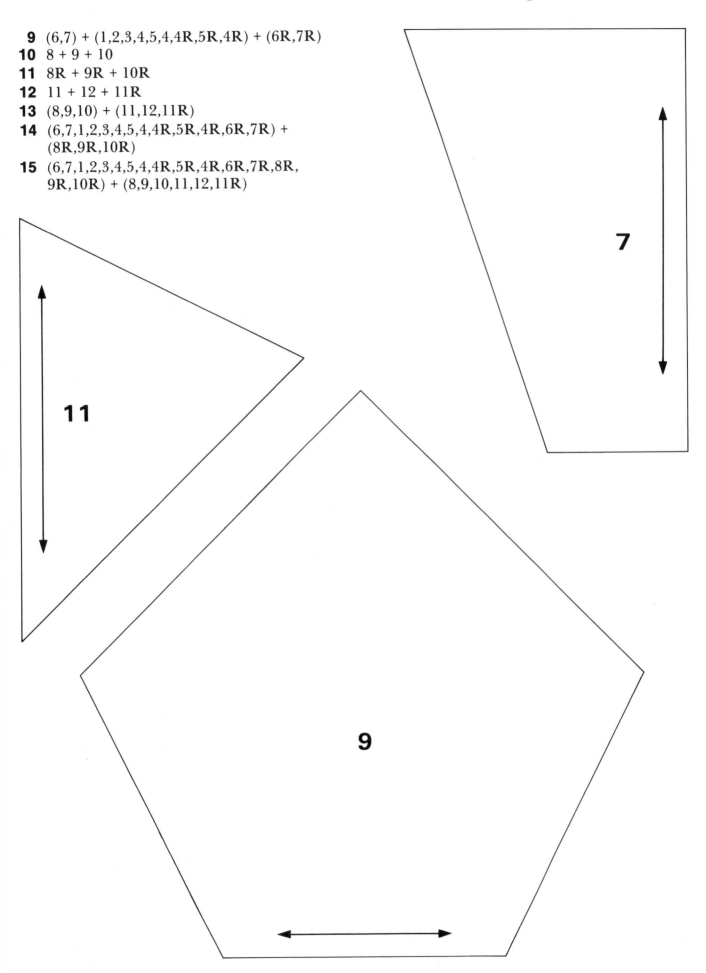

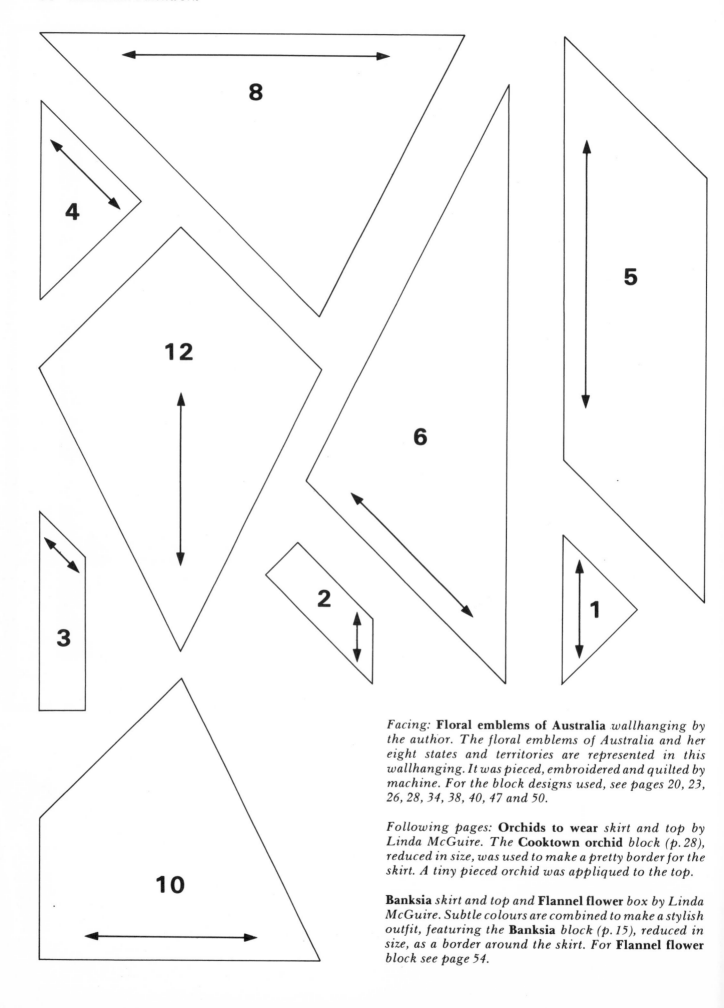

Facing: **Floral emblems of Australia** *wallhanging by the author. The floral emblems of Australia and her eight states and territories are represented in this wallhanging. It was pieced, embroidered and quilted by machine. For the block designs used, see pages 20, 23, 26, 28, 34, 38, 40, 47 and 50.*

Following pages: **Orchids to wear** *skirt and top by Linda McGuire. The* **Cooktown orchid** *block (p. 28), reduced in size, was used to make a pretty border for the skirt. A tiny pieced orchid was appliqued to the top.*

Banksia *skirt and top and* **Flannel flower** *box by Linda McGuire. Subtle colours are combined to make a stylish outfit, featuring the* **Banksia** *block (p. 15), reduced in size, as a border around the skirt. For* **Flannel flower** *block see page 54.*

N.S.W. Waratah

Tas. Blue Gum

Qld. Cooktown Orchid

Vic. Pink Heath

Australia Golden Wattle

A.C.T. Royal Bluebell

W.A. Kangaroo Paw

N.T. Sturts Desert Rose

S.A. Sturts Desert Pea

Bottlebrush

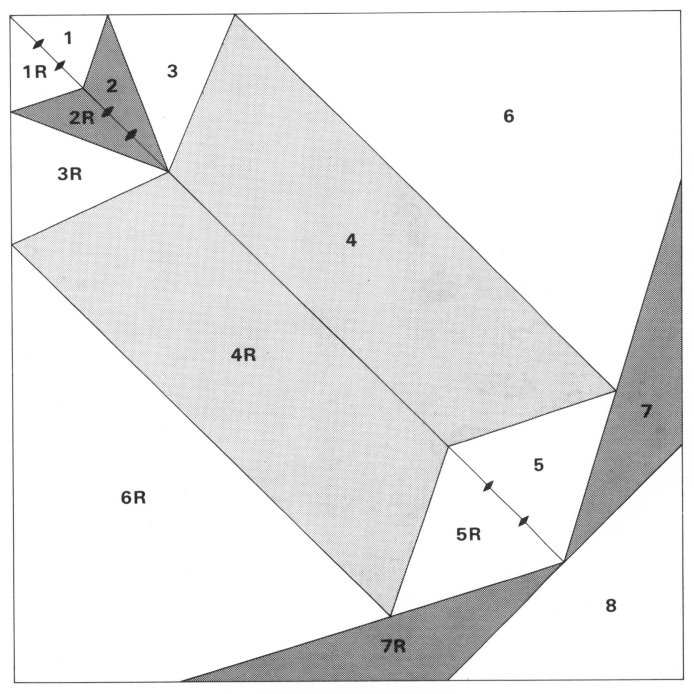

- ▨ Red, or red print
- ▧ Green
- ☐ Background

Facing: **Bottlebrush** *quilt by the author. A pretty print makes an ideal background for the brilliant* **Bottlebrush** *flowers. A star pattern is created in the centre where the blocks join. The quilt was pieced and quilted by machine.*

Piecing order

1 1 + 2 + 3 + 4 + 5
2 (1,2,3,4,5) + 6
3 (1,2,3,4,5,6) + 7
4 Repeat steps 1 to 3 with reverse pieces, i.e. 1R + 2R + 3 + 4R + 5R etc.
5 (1,2,3,4,5,6,7) + (1R,2R,3,4R,5R,6R,7R). Press this seam open to help the block lie flat.
6 Add 8 to corner to complete the block.

Note: Notches have been marked on some of the templates to help you correctly place and sew the pieces together.

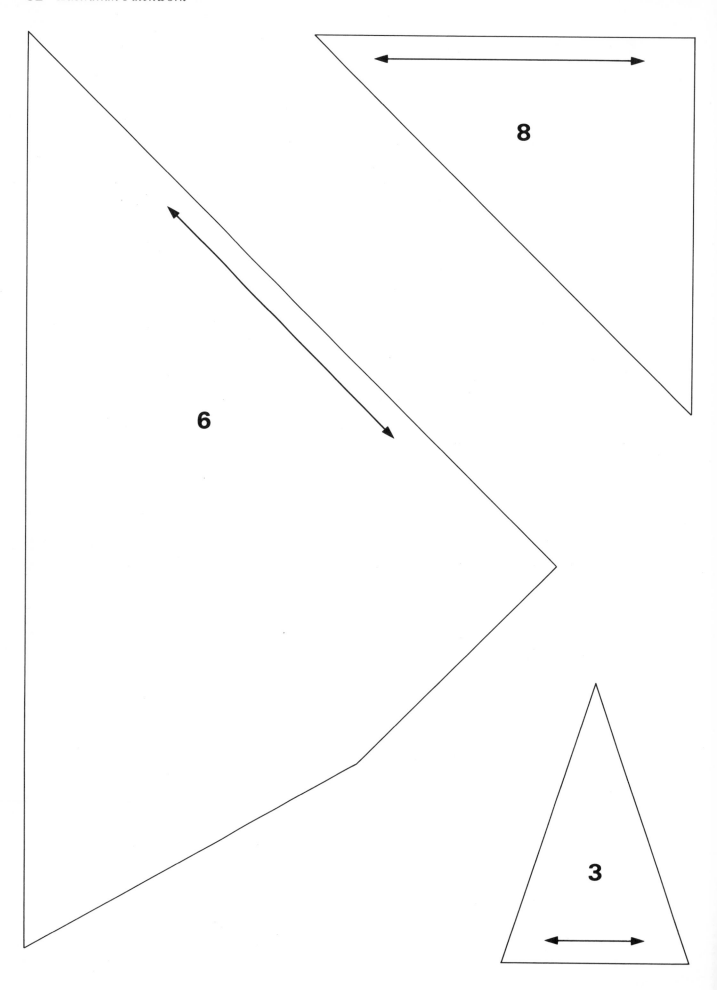

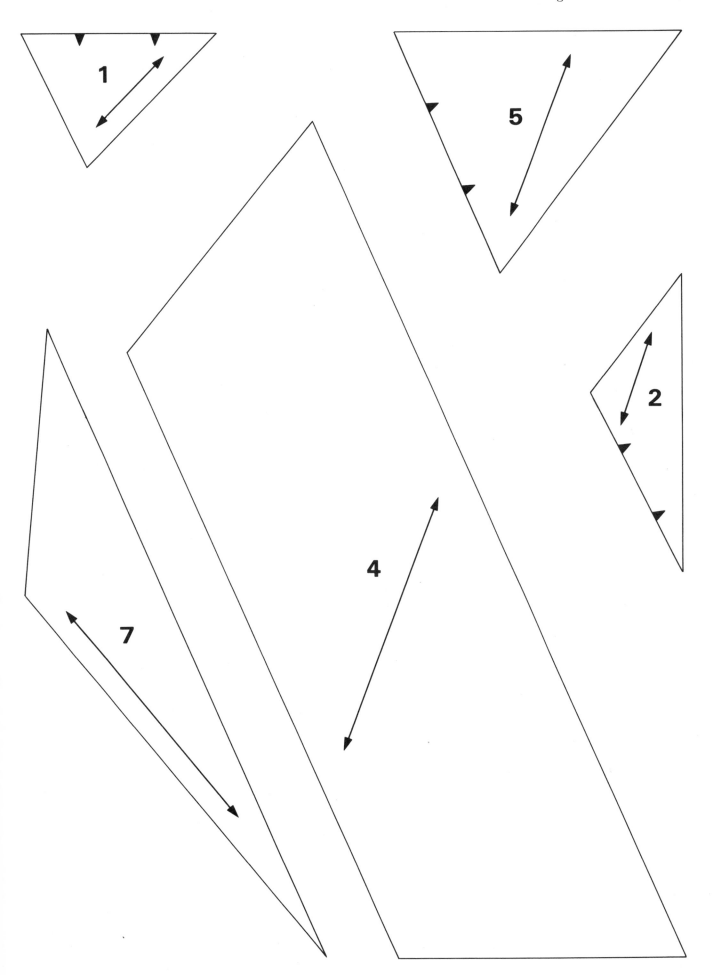

Kangaroo paw

■ Bottle green

□ Light green

▨ Red

□ Background

Note: This is an asymmetrical block, and therefore it is important to remember to turn the templates *face down* as you mark the fabric.

Piecing order

1 1 + 2 + 3
2 4 + 5 + 3
3 6 + 7 + 3
4 11 + (1,2,3) + 8 + (4,5,3) + 9 + (6,7,3) + 10 +3
5 12 + 13
6 (11,1,2,3,8,4,5,3,9,6,7,3,10,3) + (12,13)
7 Add 14 to complete the block.

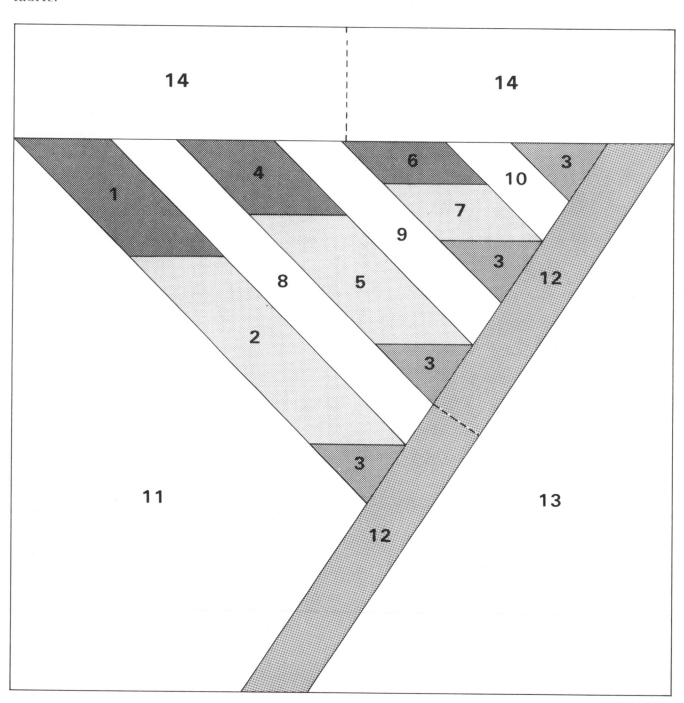

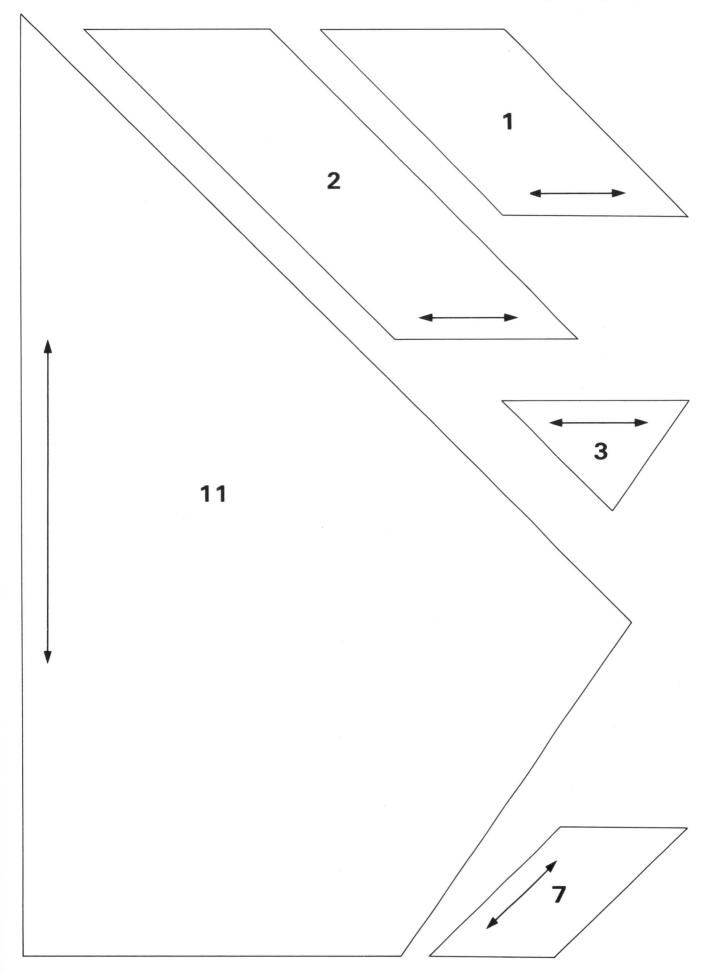

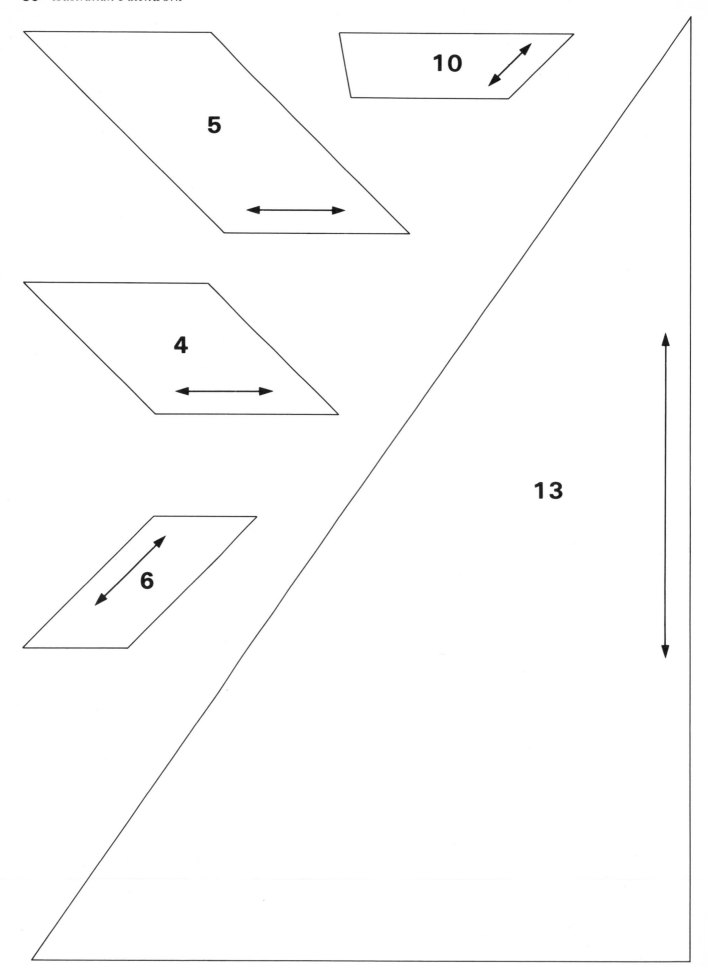

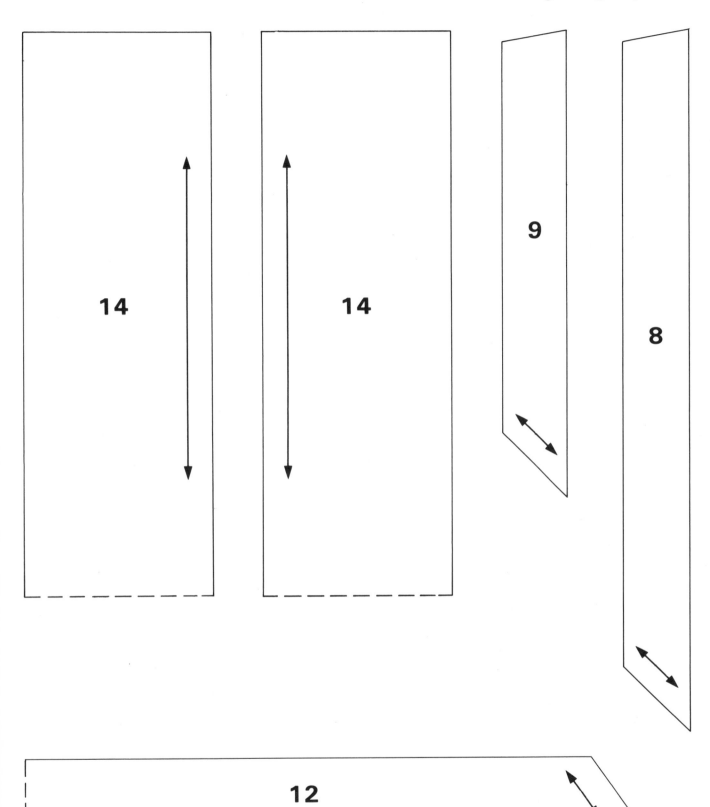

Wattle

designed by Philip Rolfe

▨ Yellow

▨ Green

☐ Background

Note: The four squares that make this block can be arranged in several different ways to create other possible designs.

Piecing order

1 1 + 2

2 Set in piece 3 to pieces 1 and 4 as follows:
- sew 3 to 1, stopping exactly at the point where 1,3 and 4 meet, and taking a few back stitches (do not sew into the seam allowance);
- sew 4 to 1, again sewing exactly to the point where 1,3 and 4 meet, and making a few back stitches;
- sew 3 to 4, sewing exactly to the point where 1,3 and 4 meet, beginning with a few back stitches just before the point.

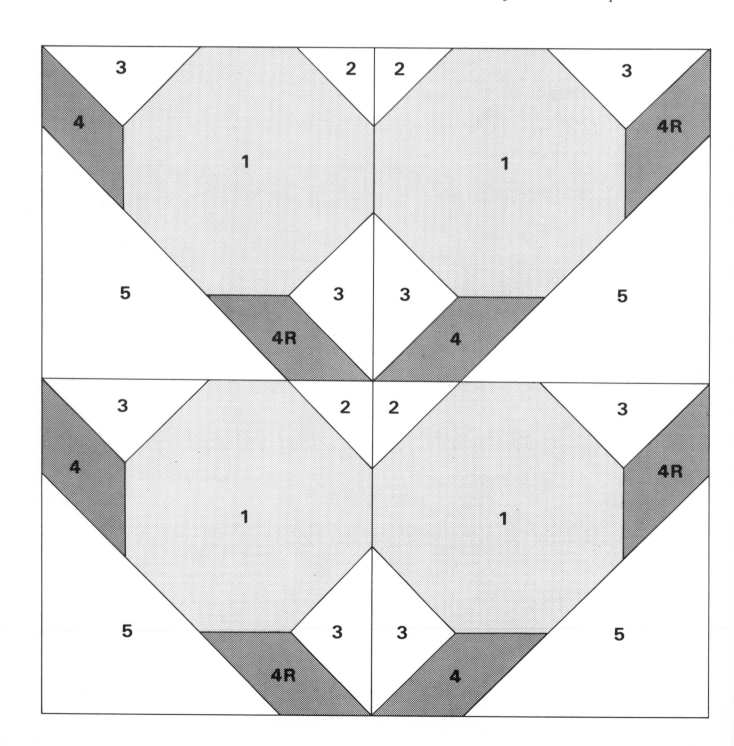

3 Repeat step 2 with 4R, i.e., set in 3 to 1 and 4R in the same way as 4 was set in.

4 (1,2,3,4,3,4R) + 5

5 Repeat steps 1 to 4 three more times to make four identical squares. Join the squares together to complete the block as shown.

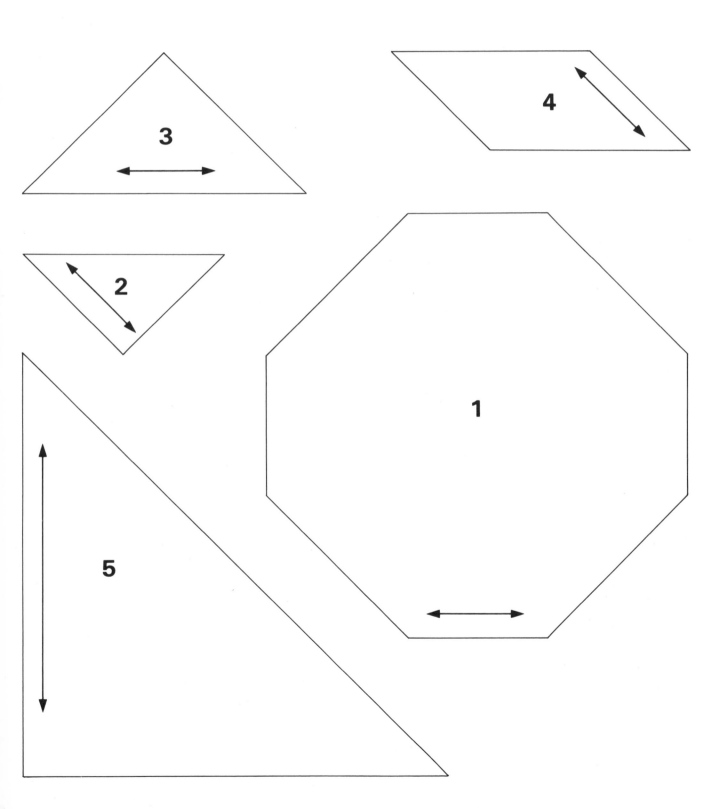

Royal bluebell

■ White

■ Blue purple, blue, or lavender

■ Green

□ Background

Note: The petal pieces of this flower are cut with the straight grain of the fabric going through the centre of each petal.

Piecing order

1 2 + 1 + 2R
2 1 + 3
3 (1,3) + 4
4 1 + 3R
5 (1,3R) + 4R
6 1 + 5
7 (1,5) + 6
8 1 + 5R
9 (1,5R) + 6R
10 Join these five segments together to make the flower, *sewing only to the points*

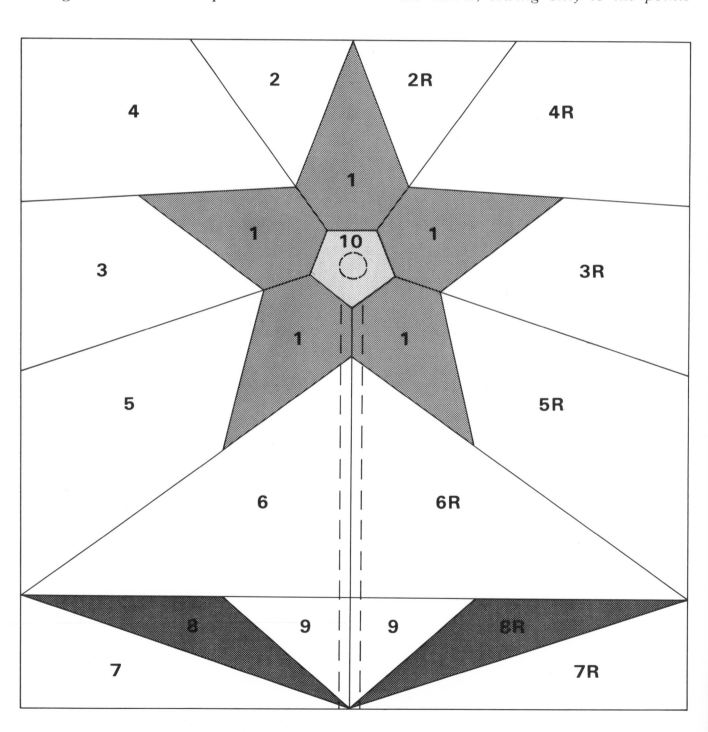

marked with crosses on the petal template (that is, do not sew into the seam allowance). End the stitching at these points with a couple of back stitches. Pin and sew these seams carefully, so that the block will lie flat. Press the seams open, and fold and press back the seam allowances at the centre.

11 7 + 8 + 9
12 7R + 8R + 9
13 (7,8,9) + (7R,8R,9)
14 Join the leaf section to the flower section of the block.

15 Applique piece 10 behind the centre of the flower. Applique a small circle of yellow to the centre of the flower. Cut a strip of green fabric 2 cm (¾″) wide, press a narrow seam allowance down each side, and applique in place as a stem, folding the top neatly into a V shape to fit between the lower petals.

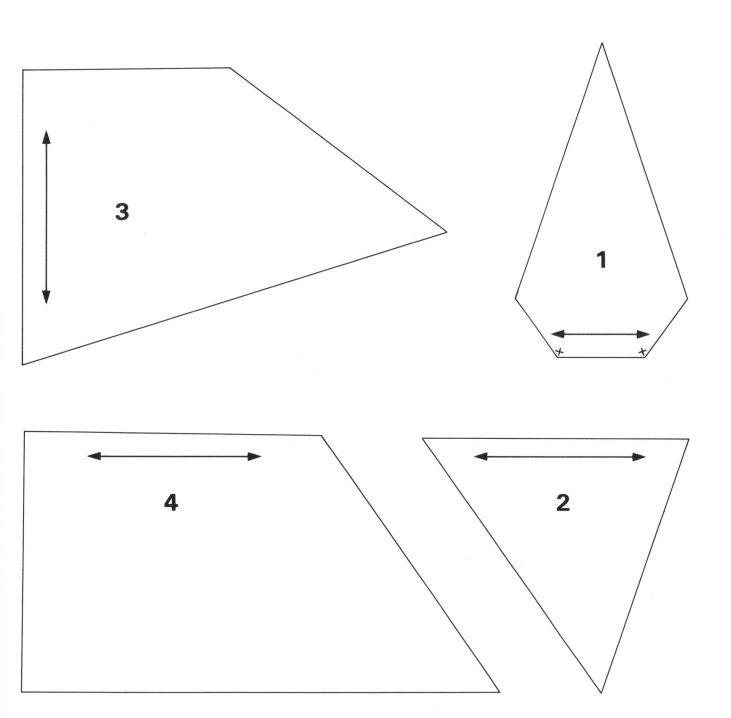

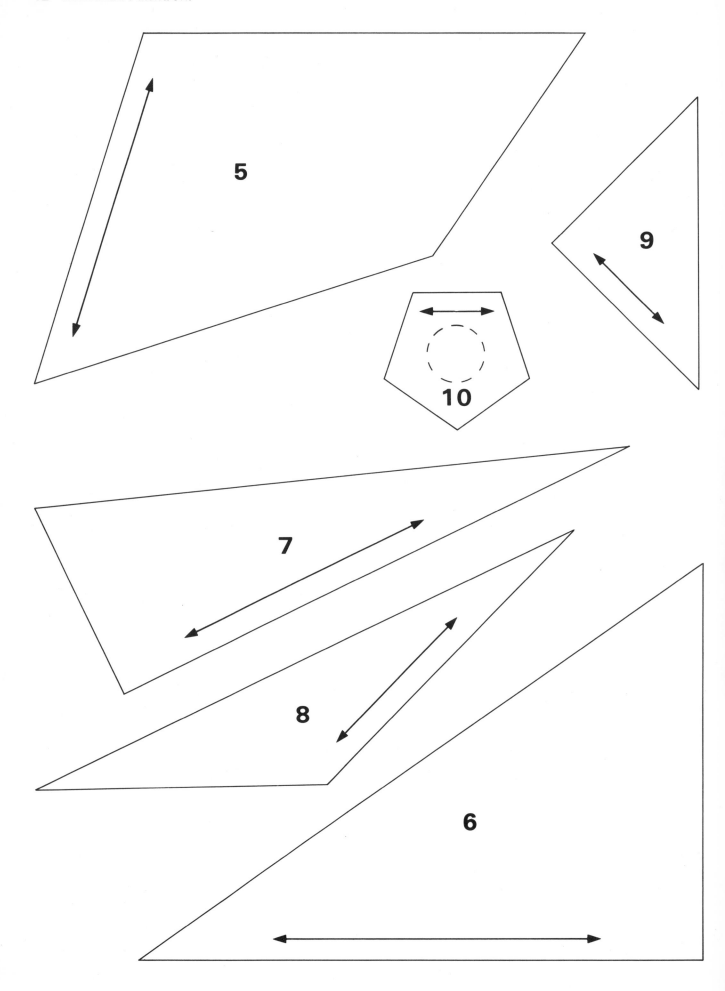

Gumnut border design

Designed by Bernie Rolfe

▨ Green

▨ Brown

☐ Background

Finished Size: 6 cm x 30 cm (2½″ x 12″)

Piecing order

1 2 + 1 + 2R
2 3 + (2,1,2R) + 3R
3 4 + (3,2,1,2R,3R) + 4R
4 Repeat steps 1, 2 and 3.
5 Join the two halves together, and press this seam open.

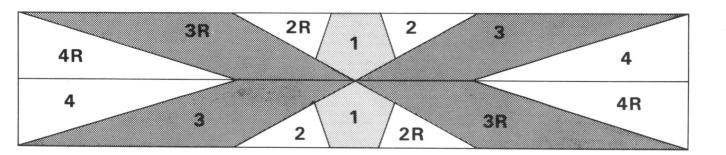

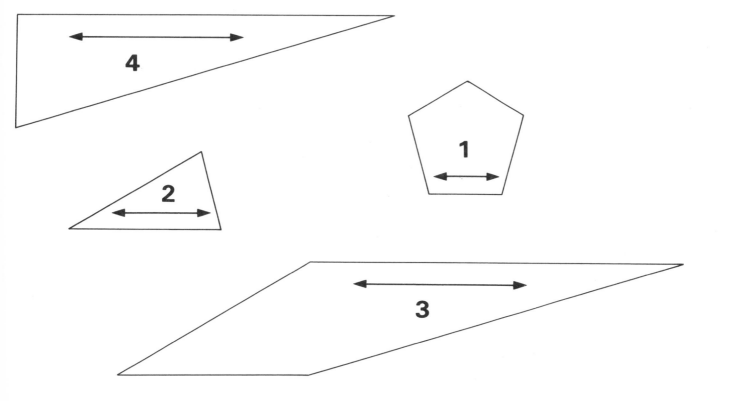

Christmas bells

- ▨ Red
- ▥ Yellow
- ☐ Background

Note: The grain of the fabric runs straight through the centre of each of the flowers in this block. Notches have been marked on some of the templates to help you correctly place and sew the pieces together. Mark the notches on the seam line, and align them when you are sewing the seam.

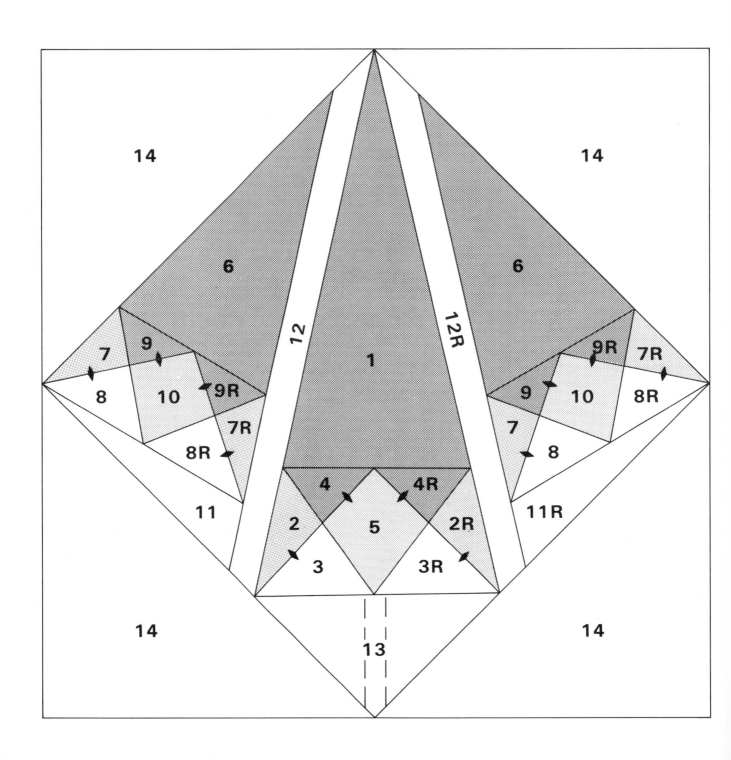

Piecing order

1 2 + 3
2 2R + 3R
3 4 + 5 + 4R
4 (2,3) + (4,5,4R) + (2R,3R)
5 1 + (2,3,4,5,4R,2R,3R)
6 7 + 8
7 7R + 8R
8 9 + 10 + 9R
9 (7,8) + (9,10,9R) + (7R,8R)
10 6 + (7,8,9,10,9R,7R,8R) + 11

11 Repeat steps 6 through to 10 to make a second flower, except that instead of adding piece 11, add piece 11R.

12 Join the three flowers together by adding 12 and 12R between them.

13 Add 13 to the base of the block.

14 Add 14 to all four corners.

15 If a stem is desired, cut a narrow strip of green fabric 2 cm (¾″) wide, press under a narrow seam allowance each side, and applique down the centre of piece 13.

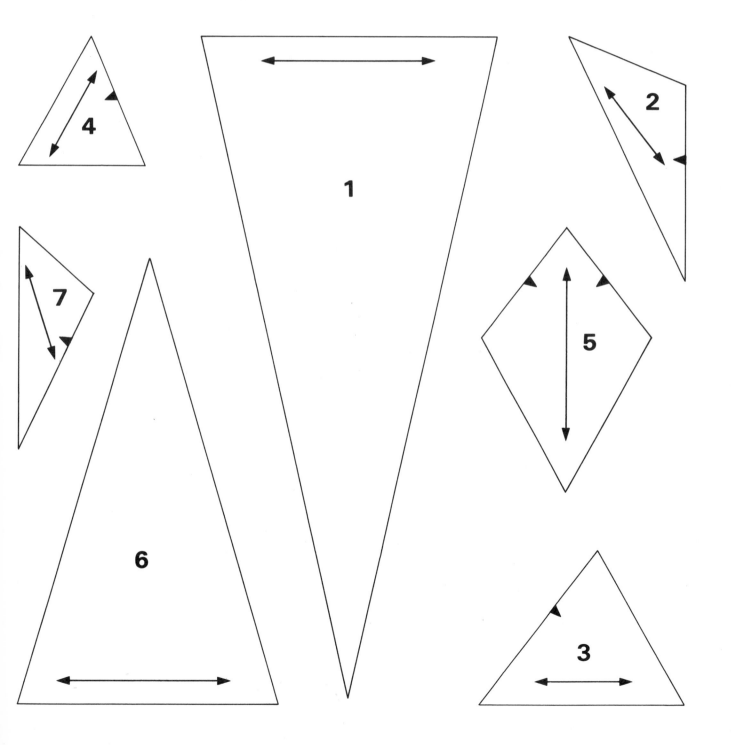

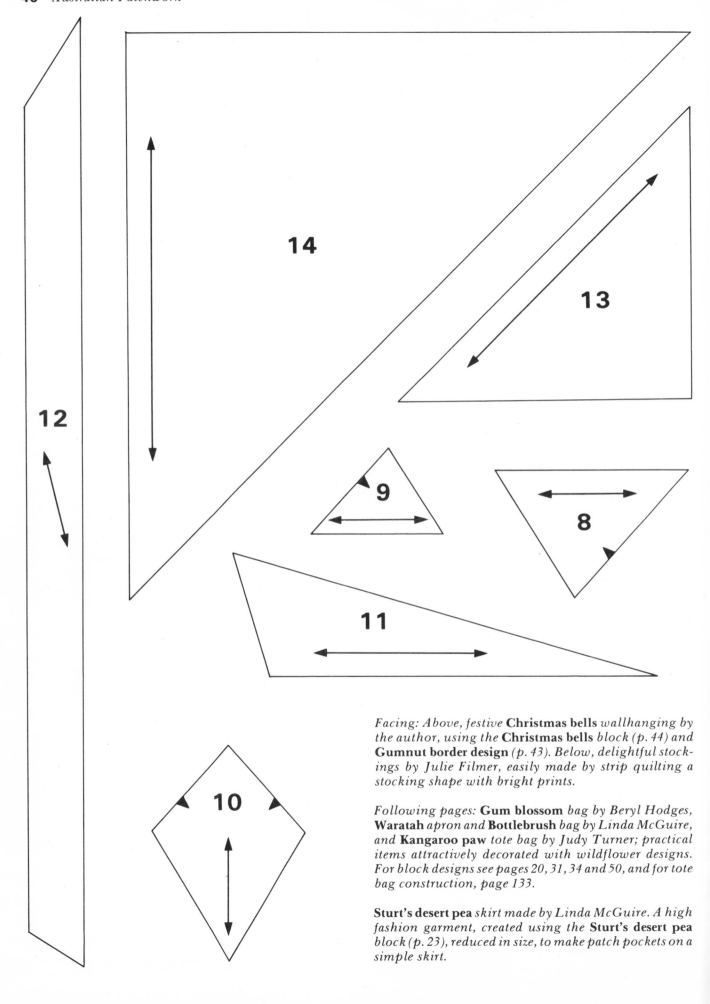

Facing: Above, festive **Christmas bells** *wallhanging by the author, using the* **Christmas bells** *block (p. 44) and* **Gumnut border design** *(p. 43). Below, delightful stockings by Julie Filmer, easily made by strip quilting a stocking shape with bright prints.*

Following pages: **Gum blossom** *bag by Beryl Hodges,* **Waratah** *apron and* **Bottlebrush** *bag by Linda McGuire, and* **Kangaroo paw** *tote bag by Judy Turner; practical items attractively decorated with wildflower designs. For block designs see pages 20, 31, 34 and 50, and for tote bag construction, page 133.*

Sturt's desert pea *skirt made by Linda McGuire. A high fashion garment, created using the* **Sturt's desert pea** *block (p. 23), reduced in size, to make patch pockets on a simple skirt.*

Pink heath

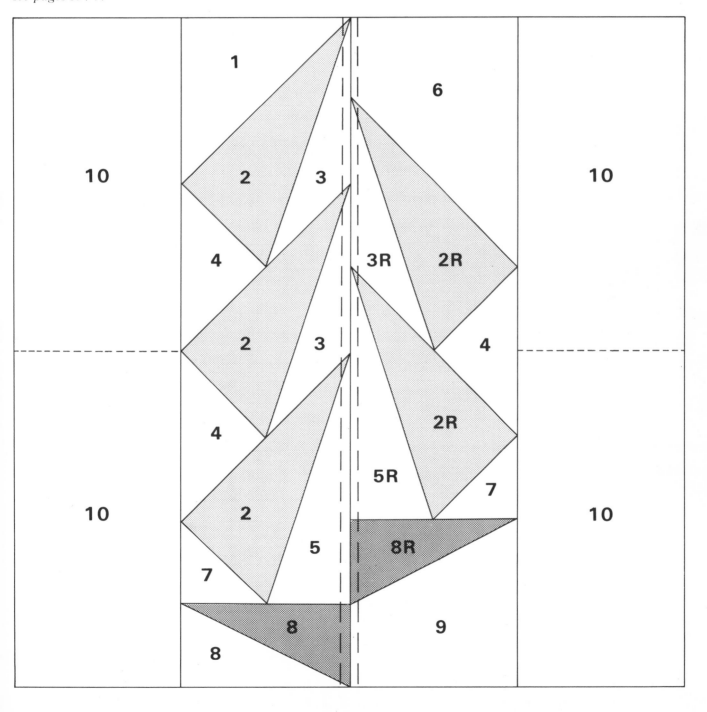

▨ Pink

▨ Green

☐ Background

Facing: **Pink heath** *vest by Beryl Hodges, along with* **Cooktown orchid** *(p. 28),* **Royal bluebell** *(p. 40), and* **Purple flag** *(p. 18) cushions by Judy Turner. Soft colours and subtle tonings were used to make an attractive vest and cushions. For cushion construction see pages 134-5.*

Piecing order

1 1 + 2
2 4 + (1,2) + 3
3 4 + 2 + 3
4 7 + 2 + 5
5 8 green + 8 background
6 (4,1,2,3) + (4,2,3) + (7,2,5) + (8,8)
7 6 + 2R
8 4 + (6,2R) + 3R
9 7 + 2R + 5R
10 8R + 9
11 (4,6,2R,3R) + (7,2R,5R) + (8R,9)

Continued overleaf

12 (4,1,2,3,4,2,3,7,2,5,8,8) + (4,6,2R,3R,7,2R, 5R,8R,9) Press this seam open.

13 Add the two 10 pieces to each side.

14 To make a stem, cut a strip of green fabric 2 cm (¾″) wide, press under a narrow seam allowance on each side, and applique along the centre of the block.

Note: This block can be varied by omitting the two 10 pieces, and repeating flowers instead. It is an asymmetrical block, so remember to turn the templates *face down* as you mark the fabric.

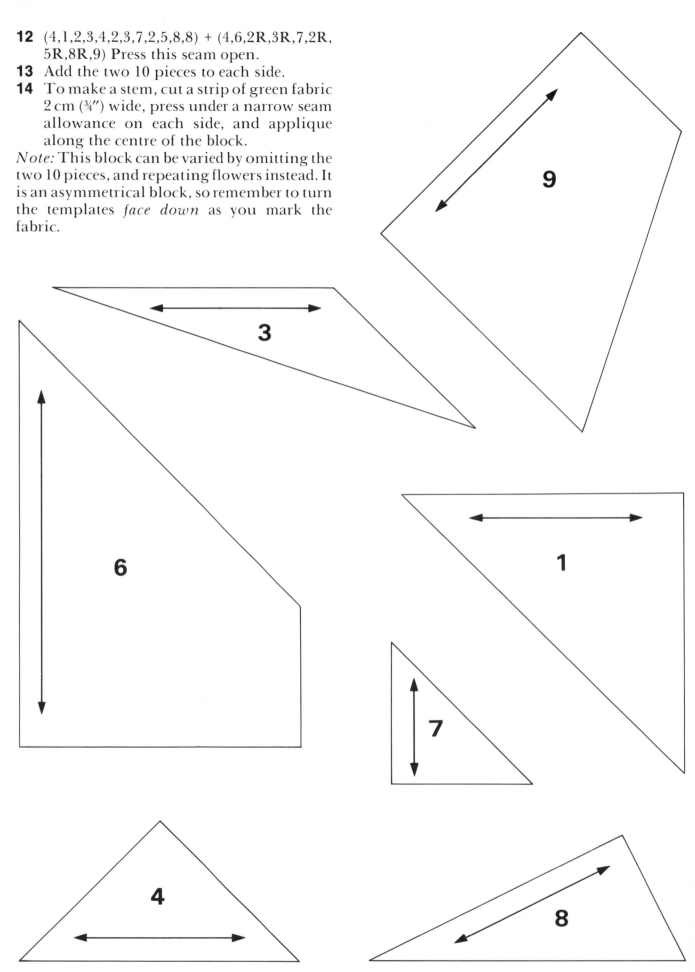

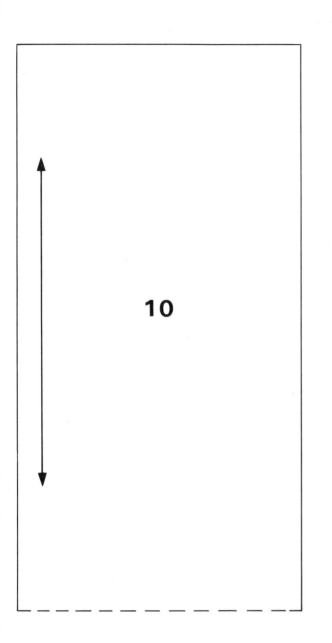

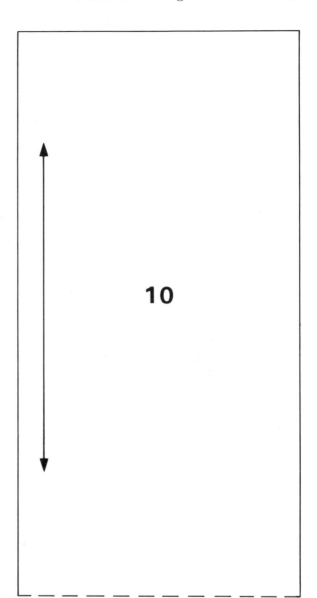

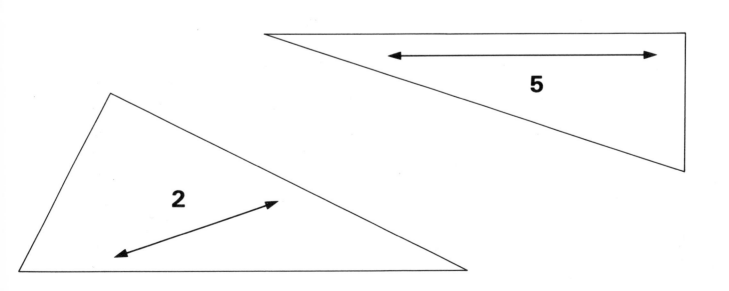

Gum blossom

■ Red, or pink, or salmon, or white

□ Light green

■ Green, or olive green

□ Background

Note: As this block involves curved seams it is helpful to first read the section on curved piecing (see p. 12). This is also an asymmetrical block, and therefore it is important to remember to turn the templates *face down* as you mark the fabric.

Piecing order

1 2 + 3 + 4
2 6 + 7 + 8 + 9 + 10
3 11 + 12 + 13 + 14 + 15
4 17 + 18
5 At this point make sure that all the seams on the curved edges are trimmed to an even 6 mm (¼″). Use the marked notches as

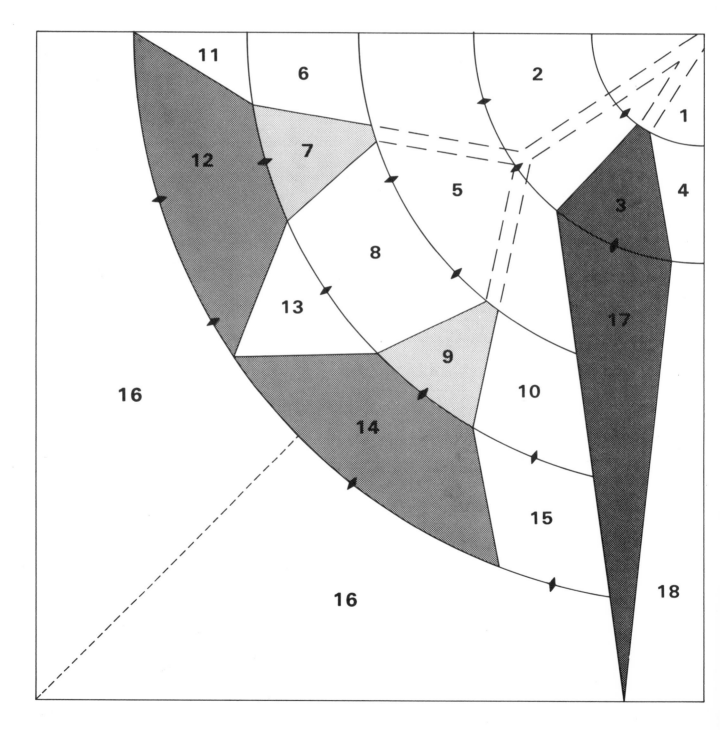

a guide for pinning the curved seams accurately.

6 1 + (2,3,4)

7 5 + (6,7,8,9,10) + (11,12,13,14,15) + 16

8 (5,6,7,8,9,10,11,12,13,14,15,16) + (17,18)

9 (1,2,3,4) + (5,6,7,8,9,10,11,12,13,14,15,16, 17,18)

10 Cut a 2 cm (¾″) wide strip of bias from light green fabric. Turn under 6 mm (¼″) each side, and applique down for stems as shown by the dotted lines in the diagram.

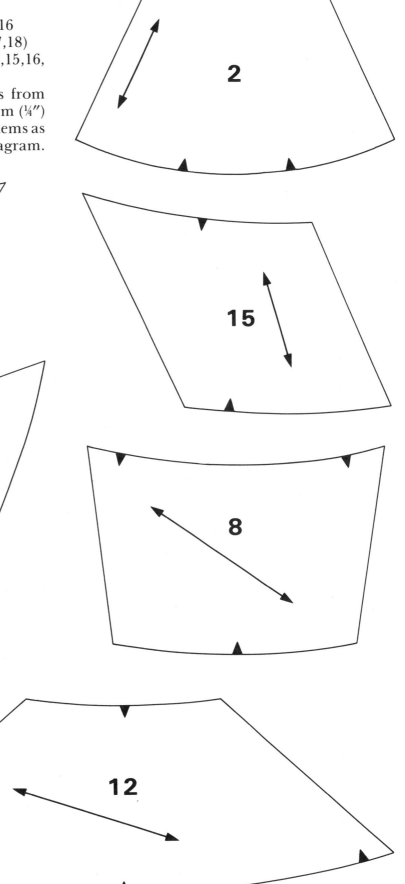

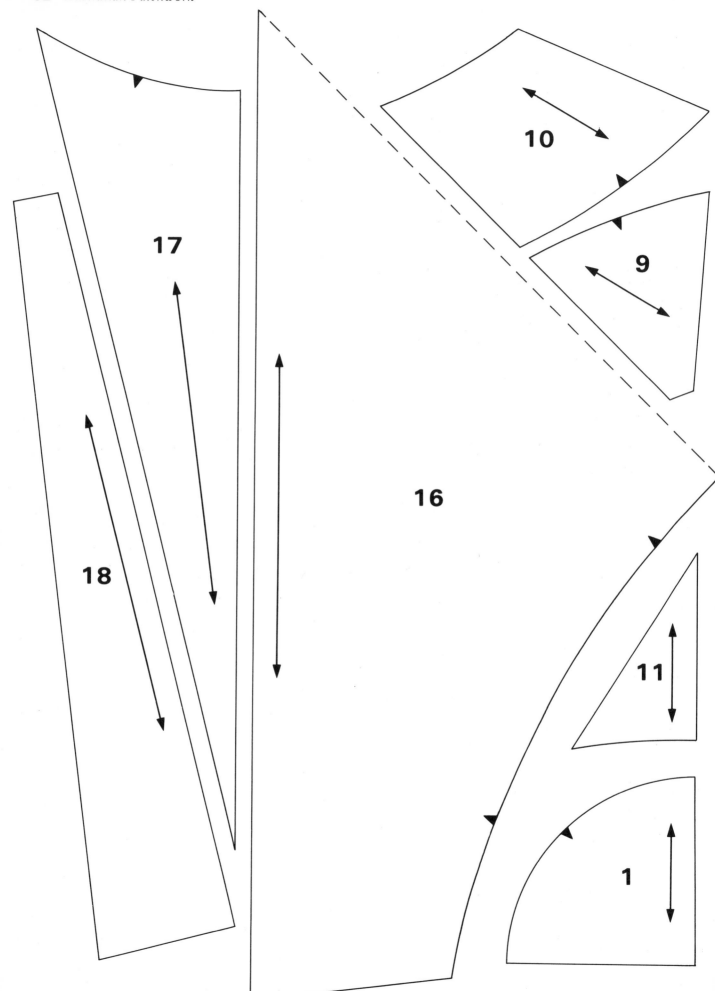

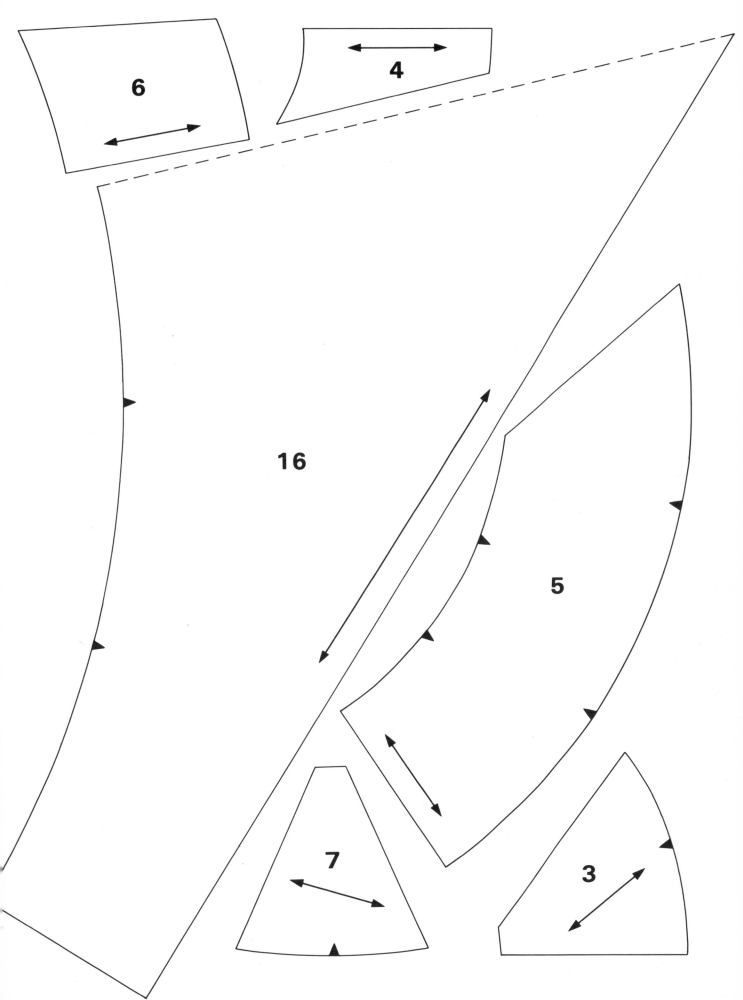

Flannel flower

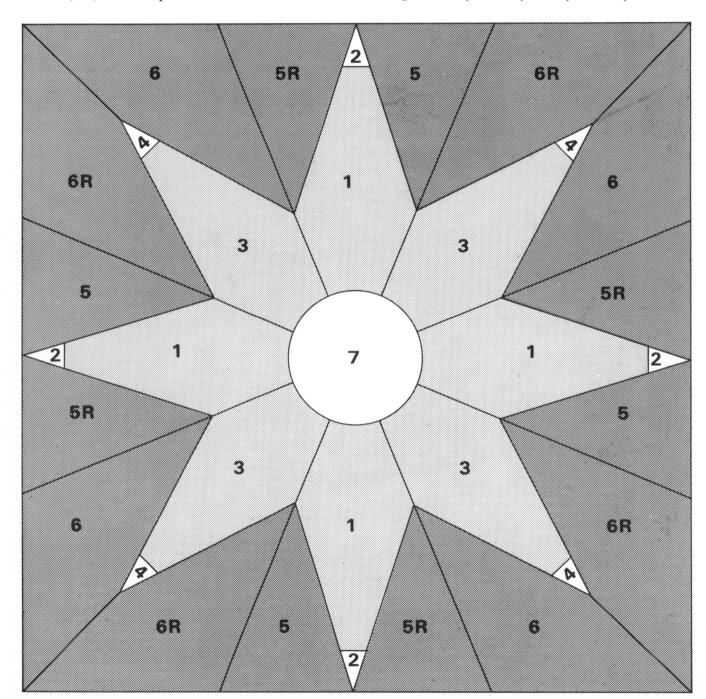

■ White or cream

□ Light green

▨ Background, or green print

Piecing order

1 1 + 2; repeat three times.
2 3 + 4; repeat three times.
3 5 + (1,2) + 5R; repeat three times.

4 Set in (3,4) to pieces 6 and 6R as follows:
* sew 6 to (3,4), sewing only to point of 4 and notch marked on 6, finishing with a few backstitches (do not sew into the seam allowance at the point of 4);
* sew 6R to (3,4,6), again sewing only to the point of 4;
* sew 6 to 6R, sewing from the point of 4 to the edge of the block.

Facing: **Flannel flower** *quilt by the author, machine pieced and quilted. Set on the diagonal,* **Flannel flower** *blocks alternate with muted green squares quilted with a design derived from the flannel flower leaf.*

5 Repeat step 4 three times.

6 Join the eight units created into a circle by joining (5,1,2,5R) to (6,3,4,6R) and so on.

7 Put a line of running stitches around the edge of 7, 3 mm (⅛″) outside the seam line. Put the template for 7 in the centre of the wrong side of piece 7, and gather the fabric around it by pulling on the circle of running stitches. Press firmly. Take out the running stitches and remove the template. Applique 7 to the centre of the block.

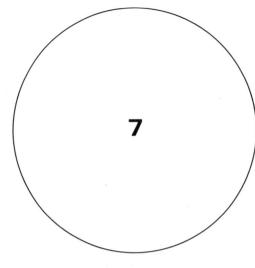

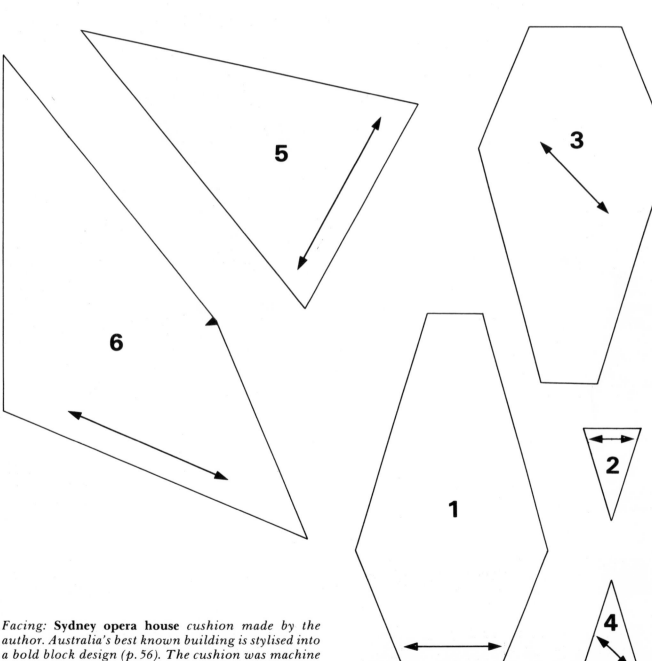

Facing: **Sydney opera house** *cushion made by the author. Australia's best known building is stylised into a bold block design (p. 56). The cushion was machine pieced and quilted.*

Sydney opera house

■ Blue

□ White

Note: As this block involves curved seams, it is helpful to first read the section on curved piecing (see p. 12). This is also an asymmetrical block, and therefore it is important to remember to turn the templates *face down* as you mark the fabric.

(see p. 12)

Piecing order

1 2 + 3
2 4 + 5
3 6 + 7
4 8 + 9
5 1 + (2,3) + (4,5) + (6,7) +(8,9) + 10
6 11 white + 12 blue + 12 white + 11 blue
7 (1,2,3,4,5,6,7,8,9,10) + (11,12,12,11)

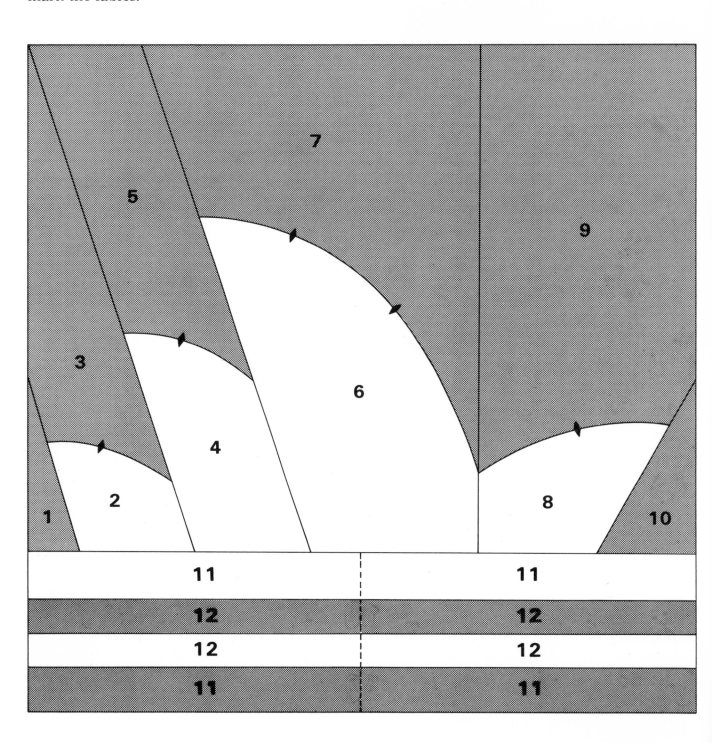

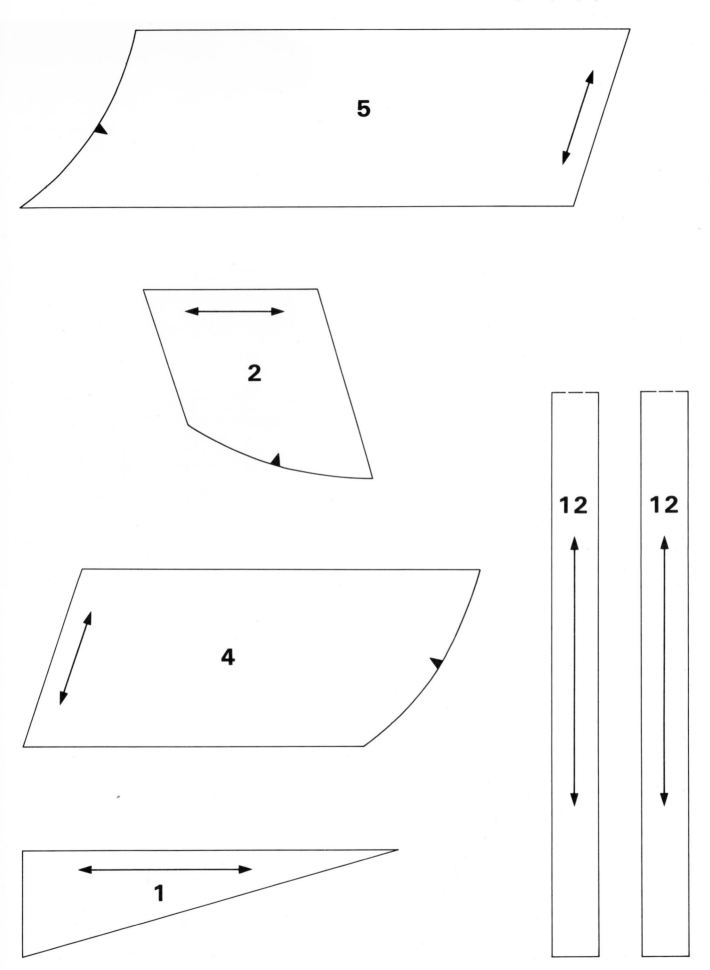

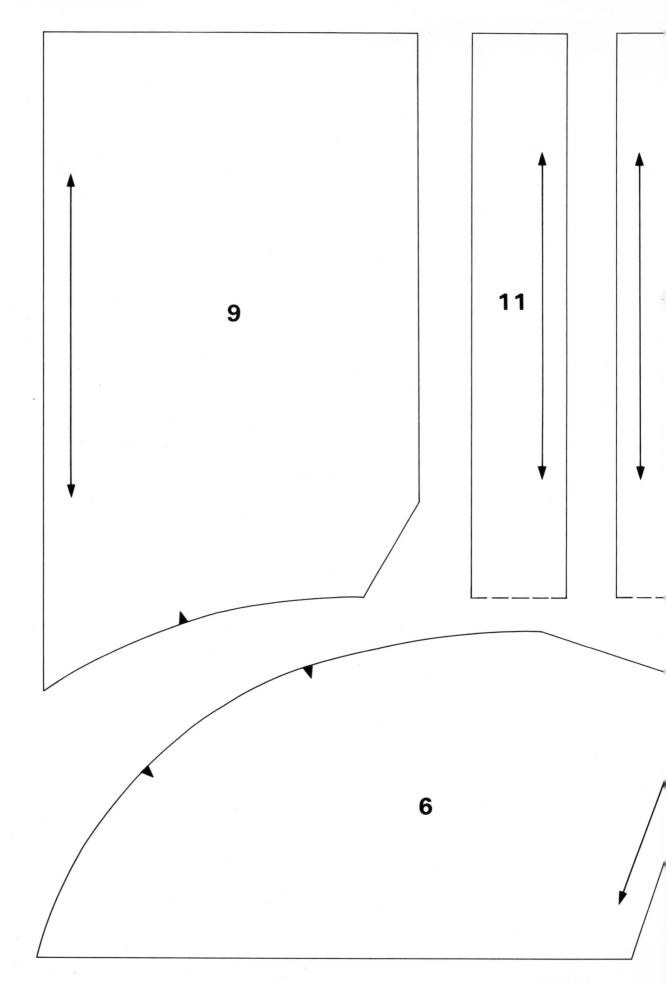

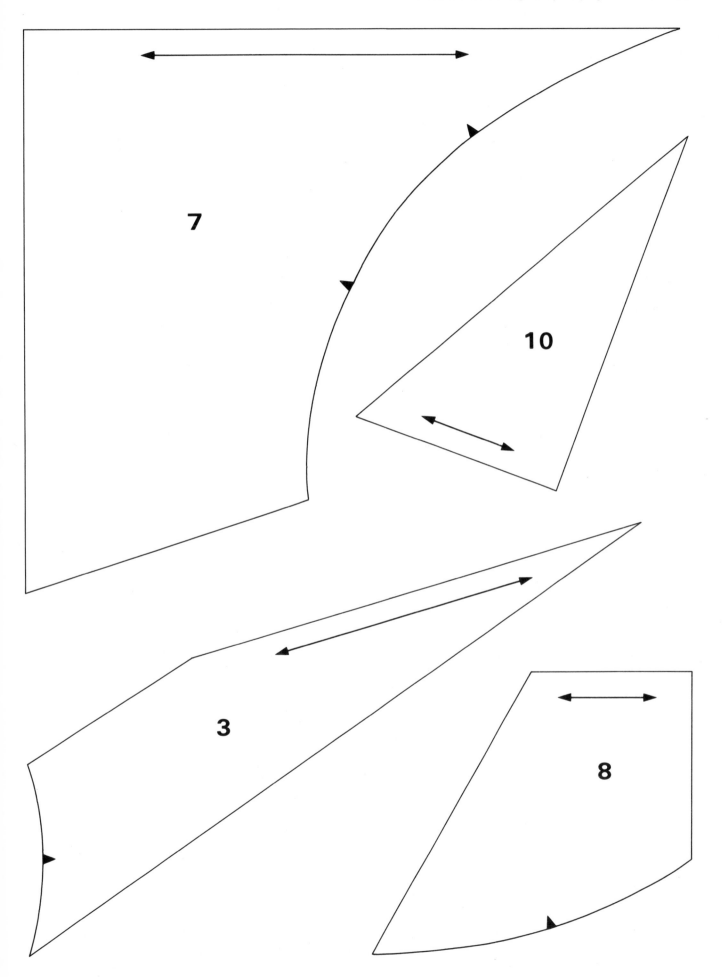

Appliqué

Applique is a technique especially suited to making curved and naturalistic designs. Its possibilities are only limited by your imagination. The wealth and singularity of Australia's flora and fauna provide wonderful design sources, and were the inspiration for my flower, bird and animal designs. One of Western Australia's unique and beautiful plants, the *Eucalyptus macrocarpa*, inspired Marjorie Coleman's applique quilt **Macrocarpa**.

Fabrics for appliqué

To applique designs from nature, such as the designs in this book, you will need a wide assortment of small pieces of fabric in different colours—both prints and plains. Try to use your prints creatively. Sometimes the most unlikely print might happen to have a little bit of the colour or pattern you want. For the colours, refer to the pictures or, better still, refer to photographs of the actual birds and flowers. Finely woven materials are best, and cotton fabrics are by far the easiest to work with. However, polypoplin and lawn can also be used. If you find a fabric that you feel you *must* use because of its colour or print, but which is too fine or open in weave, then back the fabric with *lightweight* iron-on vilene. Vilene may also be needed to back white or very pale colours, so that your background fabric does not show through. Use vilene only on the shape, and *not* on the seam allowances. Spotted fabrics can be very useful, especially for making the eyes of some of the birds. Small details can be embroidered instead of appliqued if you so desire.

How to appliqué

Step 1
Prepare the background fabric. From firm cardboard, cut a square the size of your block, plus 6 mm (¼") all around as a seam allowance —this makes a template for your background blocks. Using a sharp pencil, draw around the cardboard template on the background fabric. Be careful that the grain is correct for the block you are making.

Step 2
Copy an applique design from one of the designs in this book, enlarging the design if necessary. To enlarge a design from a grid, first take a large sheet of graph paper or ordinary paper, and mark it with a grid of 3 cm (1¼") squares (or whatever size squares you wish). Copy the design from the book, using the squares to help you draw it correctly. For the Australian bird designs, the birds themselves have been drawn full size, but you will need to use the grid to draw the backgrounds. When the design has been drawn to your satisfaction, mark over it with a black pen. This design becomes your master copy.

Step 3
Make a tracing from the master copy of your design, and mark the grain lines through each piece of the design (the grid lines will help you with this).

Step 4
Cut out all the pieces from the tracing paper— there should be a separate piece for each part of the pattern, though very small details such as eyes and claws can be left, and a separate tracing taken of them.

Step 5
Pin the tracing-paper pattern on to coloured fabric suitable for each piece, matching marked grain lines with the grain of the fabric. For applique, unless there is a special reason to do otherwise, always match the grain of the applique piece with the grain of the background fabric.

Step 6
Cut the pieces out, allowing only a 4 mm (⅛") seam allowance all around each piece *except* where one piece overlaps another. Where there

is an overlap, make an 8 mm (⅜″) seam allowance on the section of the bottom piece that goes underneath the overlapping piece.

Step 7
Leave the tracing paper patterns pinned to the fabric and, when all the pieces are cut out for the design, re-assemble them on top of the prepared background square, matching the grain lines with the grain in the background fabric. The tracing paper pieces should fit back together like a jigsaw puzzle. Pin the pieces of fabric to the background, remove the tracing paper pieces, then tack (baste) the pieces to the background. Some of the designs have pieces which need special treatment. (See 'Special techniques' below, and the specific instructions for the **Australian birds** wallhanging (p. 142) and the **Australian animals** wallhanging (p. 144).

Step 8
Using a thread that matches the piece of fabric being appliqued, stitch each piece to the background, turning under a 4 mm (⅛″) seam as you go. To make the stitching almost invisible, bring the needle out from the fold in the seam allowance, then straight down into the background, coming back up again into the fold with the next stitch, and so on. Use the needle to help you smoothly turn under the seam allowance on convex curves. On concave curves and sharp angles, you will need to nick the seam allowance with a pair of sharp scissors to allow it to turn under.

First sew the pieces that are beneath overlapping pieces, then sew the top pieces. Finally add details such as eyes.

Special techniques

Circles: To make small round circles (e.g. for wattle, or for the eyes of birds), first cut a circle of cardboard the size indicated in the design. Cut out the fabric with a 6 mm (¼″) seam allowance. Sew a small running stitch around the piece about 4 mm (⅛″) from the edge. Put the cardboard circle in the middle, then draw up the thread, gathering the fabric around the cardboard shape. Press firmly, then remove the cardboard and trim the seam allowance. The shape is now ready to sew.

Narrow strips: To make narrow strips (e.g. for stems and some bird claws), cut pieces as bias strips the required width and length, including seam allowances. These can be curved as needed. In this situation do not worry about matching the grain.

Reverse applique: In some cases, where one shape is completely surrounded by another, a technique of reverse applique can be used. Cut a hole in the fabric of the outside shape, remembering to leave the 4 mm (⅛″) seam allowance. Cut the inside shape with a generous seam allowance, and lay it behind the hole. Pin and tack (baste) in place. Applique the top fabric to the fabric underneath, making nicks in the seam allowance as necessary to turn it under.

Sharp points: Sharp points can be sewn by folding in three stages. First fold down the seam allowance up to the point, then fold over the tip of the point, finally fold down the seam allowance on the other side of the point.

Small repeating motifs: Some of the designs, such as **Pink heath** and **Wattle**, have many small shapes that are repetitive. One template can be made for all the same shapes, and the shapes of the pieces can be varied slightly as they are being sewn down.

Zigzag edges: To make zigzag edges (e.g. for some flowers), first cut the shape out with a straight edge (including the seam allowance) then, along the edge, cut nicks the depth you want the zigzags to be. As you sew, fold the fabric between the nicks into points, trimming away as necessary any extra seam allowance along the sides of the points. Make a single stitch at the deepest point of each zigzag where there is no seam allowance to turn under.

Appliqué designs
Australian birds

Pelican

1 square = 3 cm (1¼″)

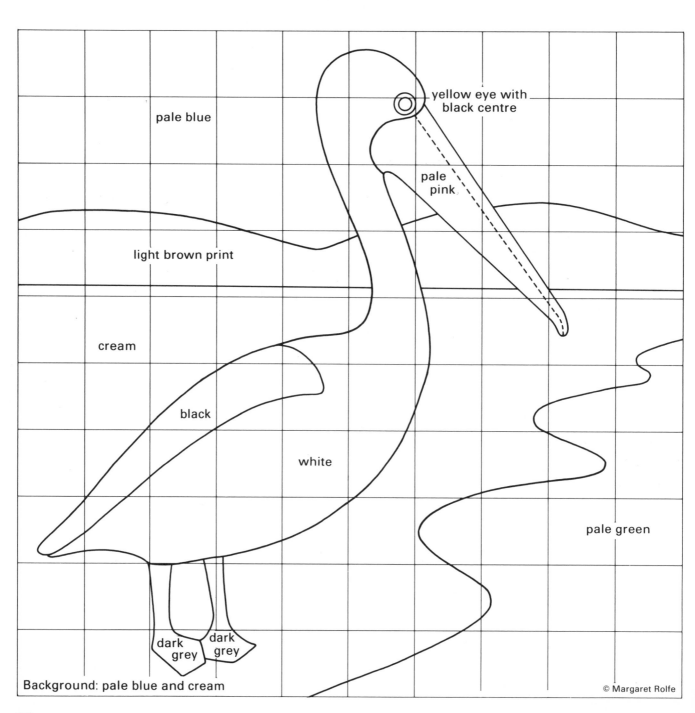

pale blue

yellow eye with
black centre

pale
pink

light brown print

cream

black

white

pale green

dark
grey

dark
grey

Background: pale blue and cream

© Margaret Rolfe

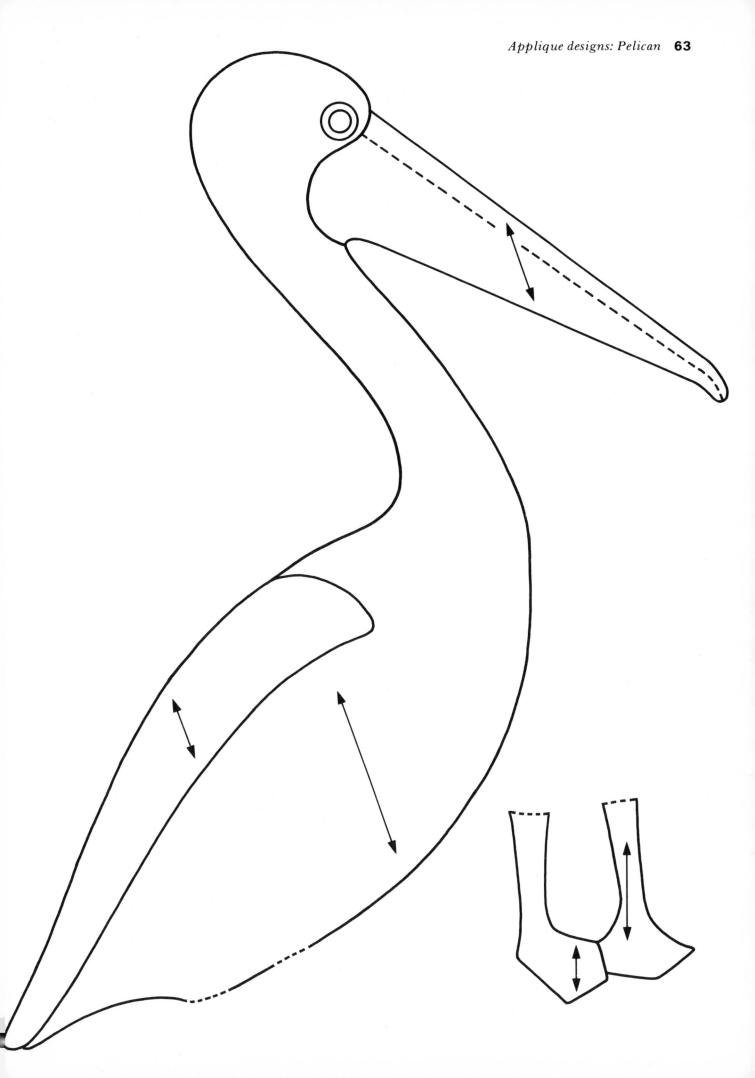

Sulphur-crested cockatoo

1 square = 3 cm (1¼")

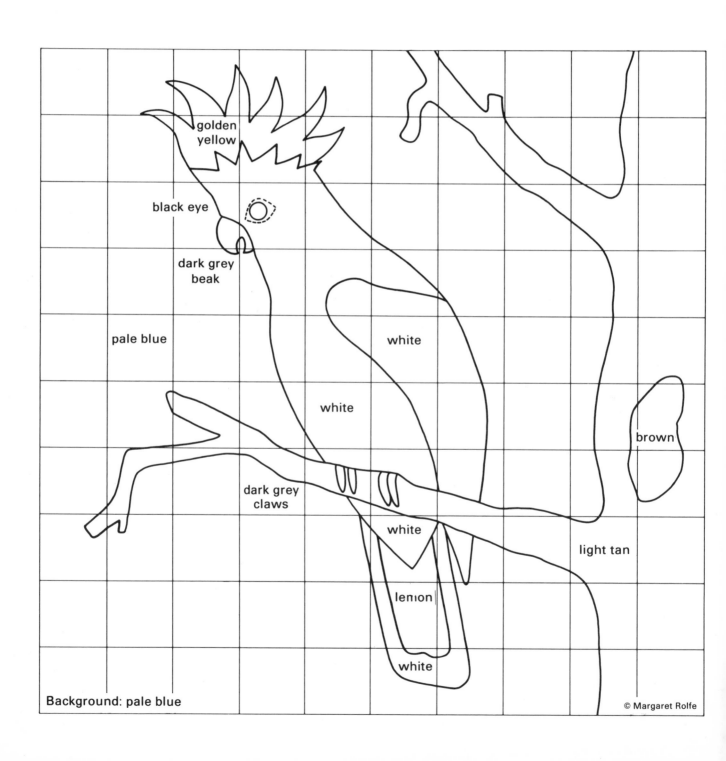

golden
yellow

black eye

dark grey
beak

pale blue

white

white

brown

dark grey
claws

white

light tan

lemon

white

Background: pale blue

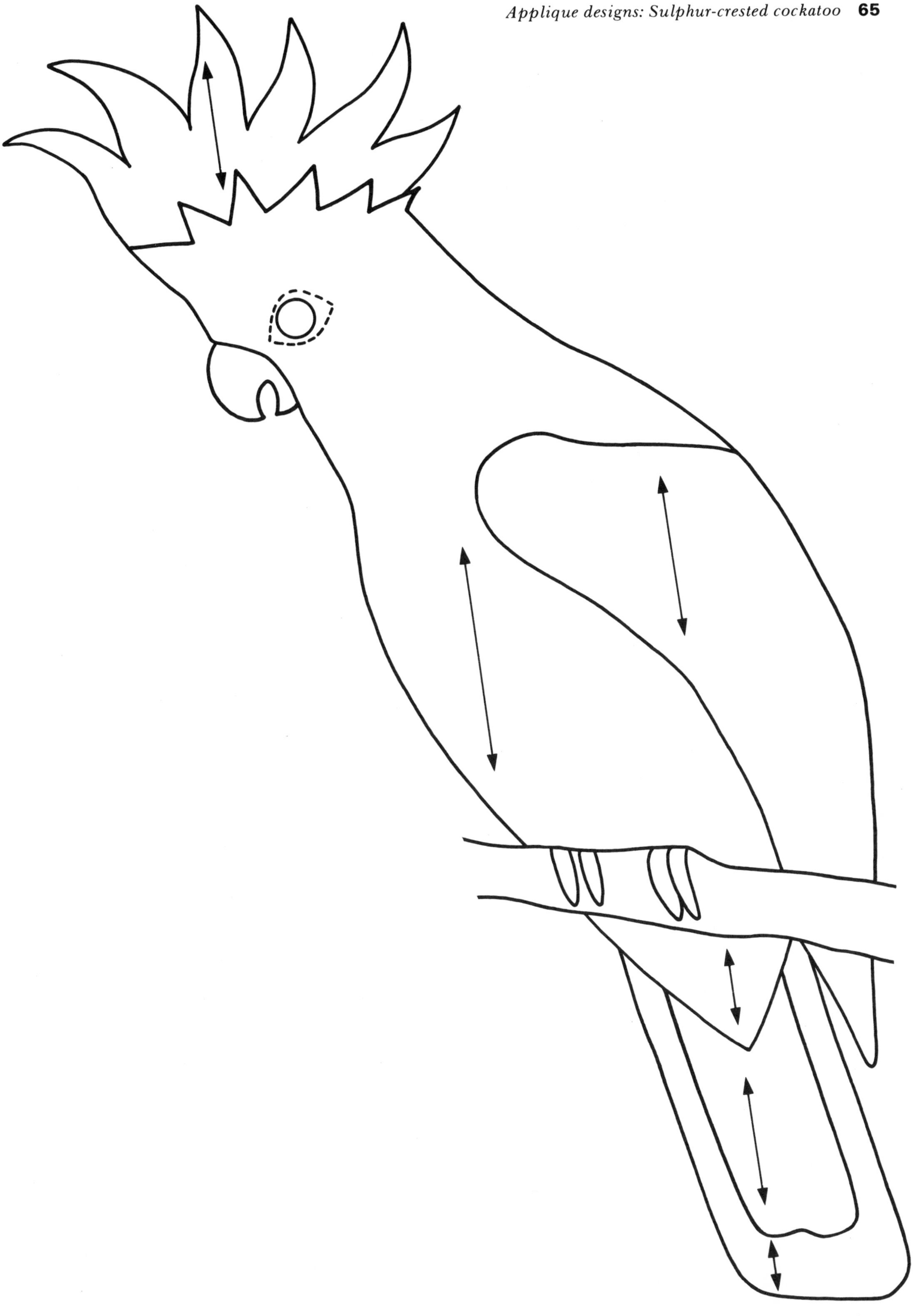

Crimson rosella

l square = 3 cm (1¼″)

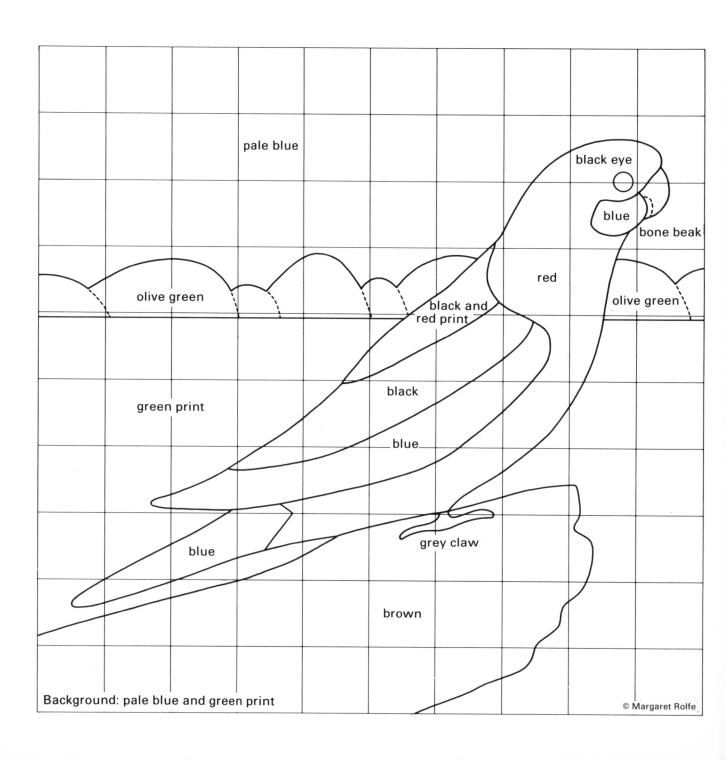

pale blue

black eye

blue

bone beak

red

olive green

olive green

black and
red print

green print

black

blue

blue

grey claw

brown

Background: pale blue and green print

© Margaret Rolfe

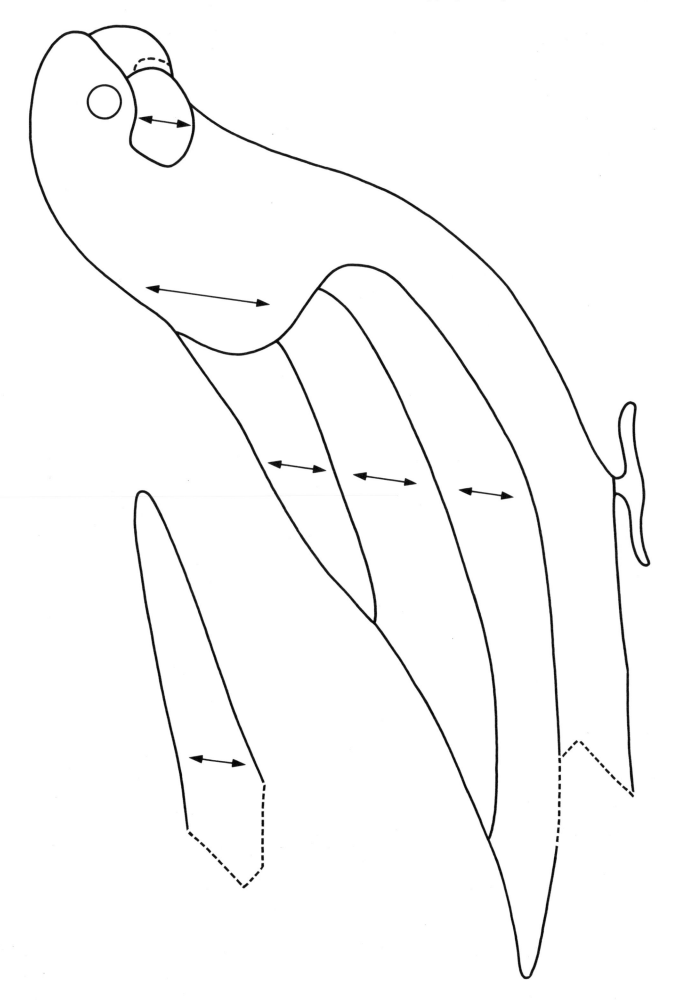

Black swan

1 square = 3 cm (1¼″)

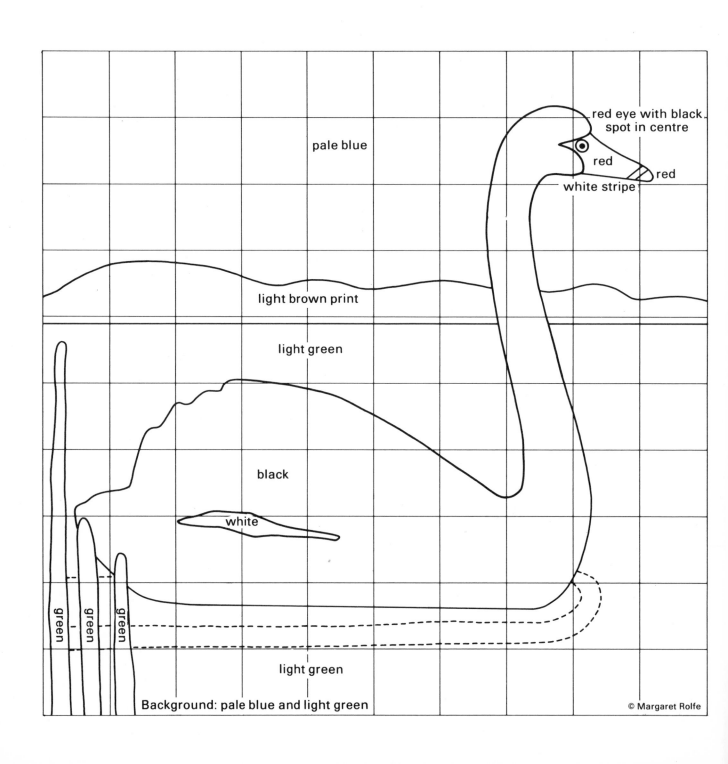

pale blue

red eye with black
spot in centre

red

red

white stripe

light brown print

light green

black

white

green

green

green

light green

Background: pale blue and light green

© Margaret Rolfe

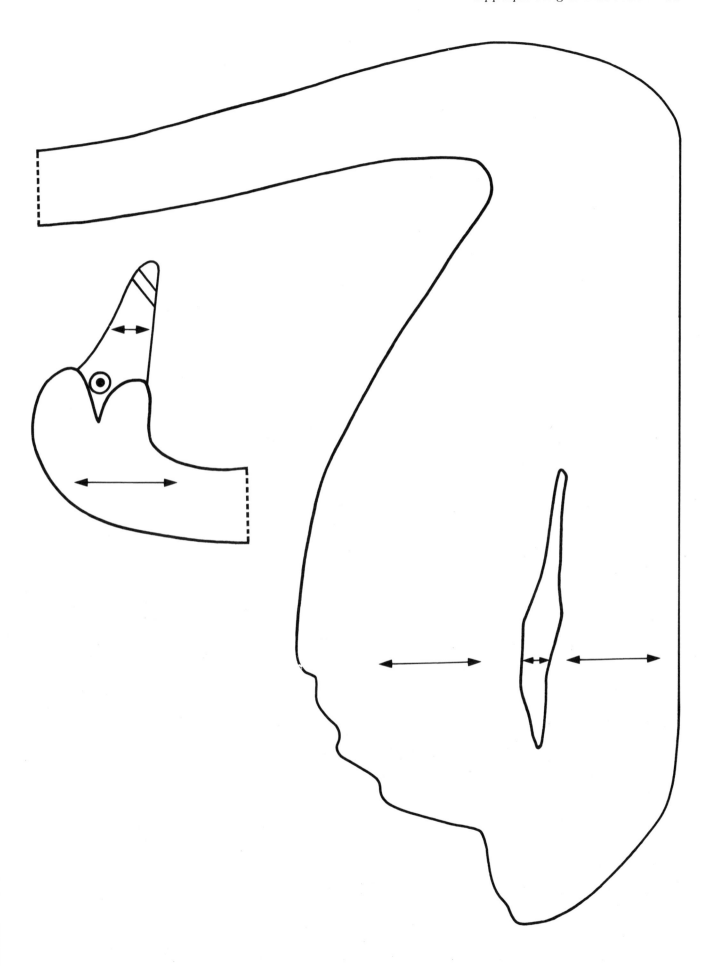

Galah

1 square = 3 cm (1¼″)

Facing: **Australian birds** *wallhanging by the author. Nine of Australia's unique and beautiful birds are pictured in this wallhanging which was appliqued and quilted by hand. For applique bird designs, see pages 62-79. For wallhanging construction see page 142.*

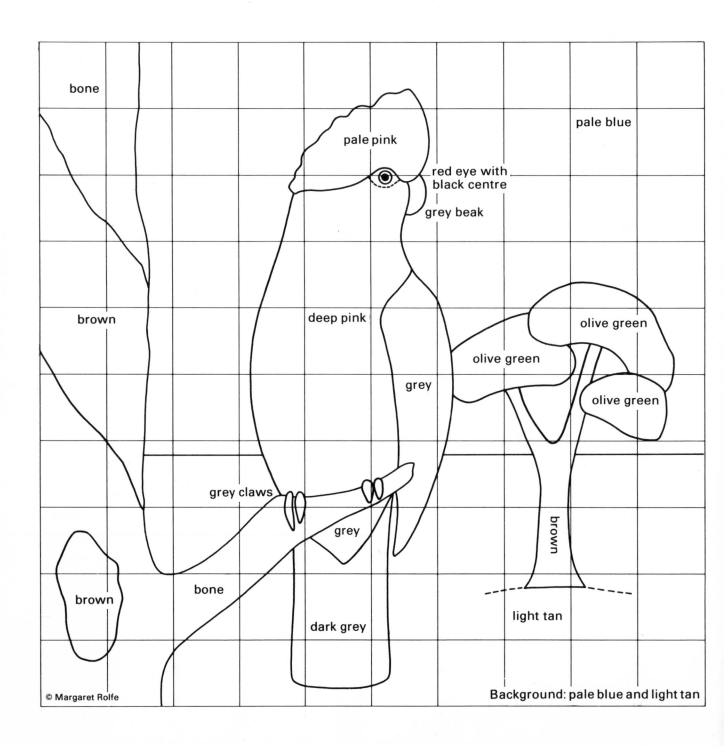

bone

pale blue

pale pink

red eye with black centre

grey beak

brown

deep pink

olive green

olive green

grey

olive green

grey claws

grey

brown

brown

bone

dark grey

light tan

© Margaret Rolfe

Background: pale blue and light tan

Step-by-step: Appliqué

Step 1 Draw or copy design so that it is full size. Copy on to tracing paper, marking grain lines on each piece.

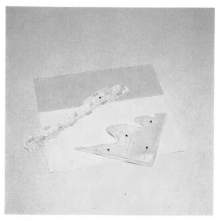

Step 2 Make background. Cut out tracing paper pieces, pin to suitable fabric. Cut out with 4 mm (⅛″) seam allowances, except where 8 mm (⅜″) required for underlap.

Step 3 Assemble the pieces on the background. Fit the tracing paper shapes back together again. Pin fabric pieces to the background, and remove paper pieces.

Step 4 Tack all the pieces to the background, keeping tacking 6 mm (¼″) away from cut edge so you can turn the seam allowance under.

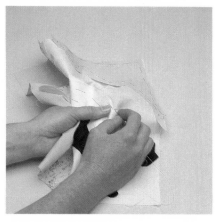

Step 5 Matching the colour of the thread to the appliqué piece, stitch the pieces to the background. Turn under 4 mm (⅛″) seam allowance as you sew.

Step 6 The finished appliqué block of the pelican from the **Australian birds** wall-hanging.

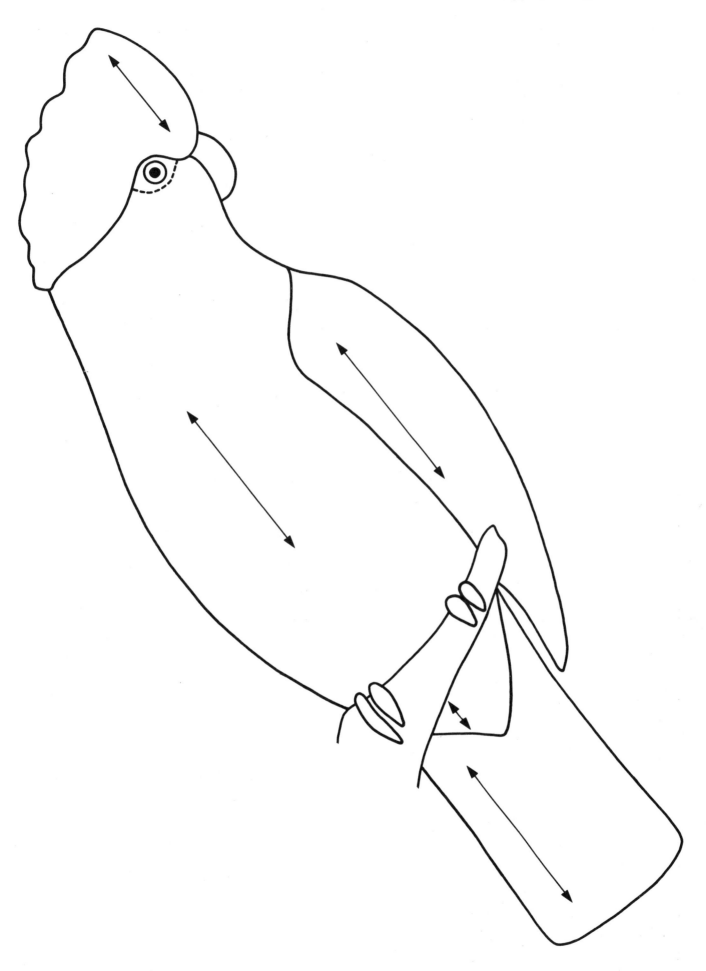

Superb blue wren

1 square = 3 cm (1¼″)

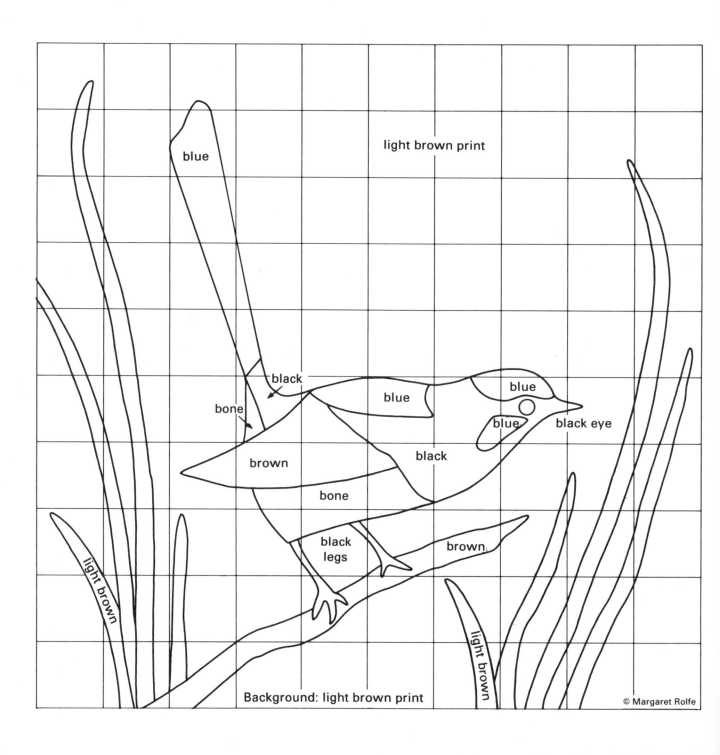

light brown print

blue

black

bone

blue

blue

blue

black eye

brown

black

bone

black legs

brown

light brown

light brown

Background: light brown print

© Margaret Rolfe

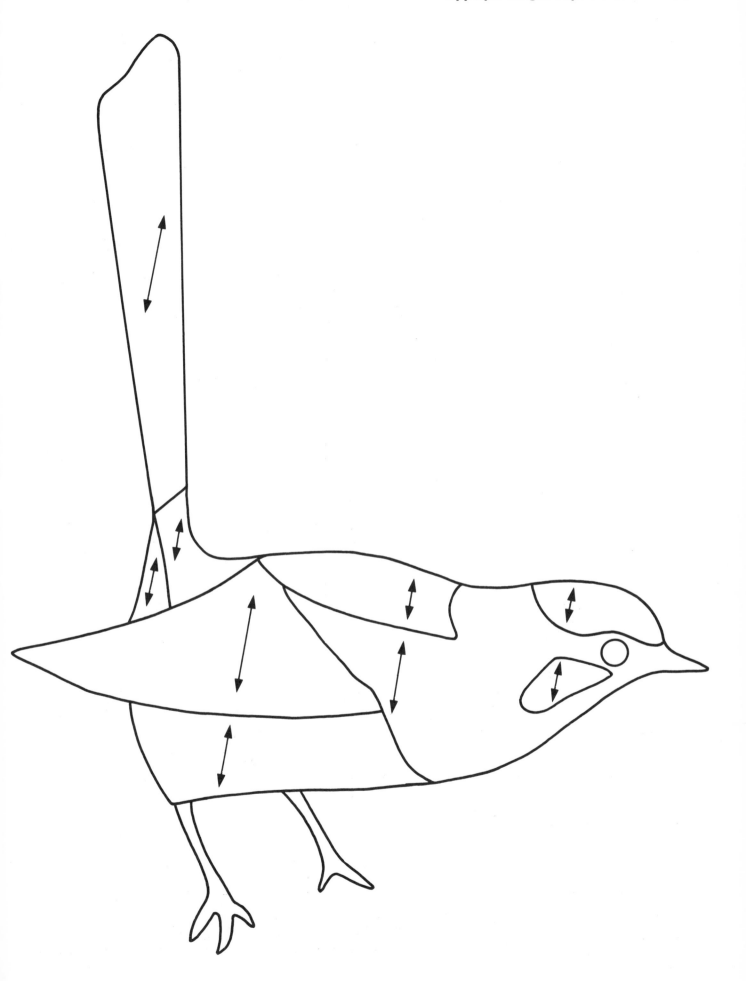

Emu

1 square = 3 cm (1¼")

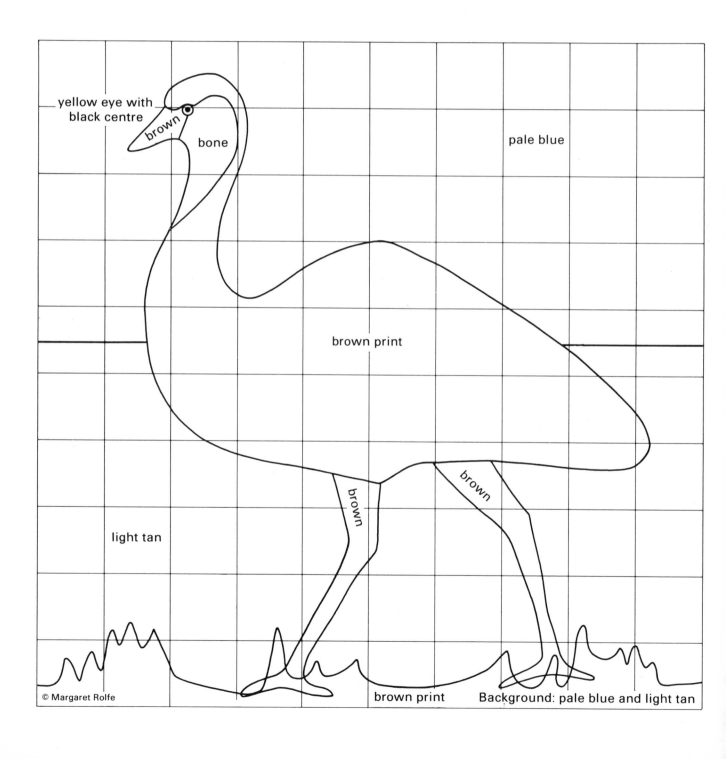

yellow eye with
black centre

brown

bone

pale blue

brown print

brown

brown

light tan

© Margaret Rolfe

brown print

Background: pale blue and light tan

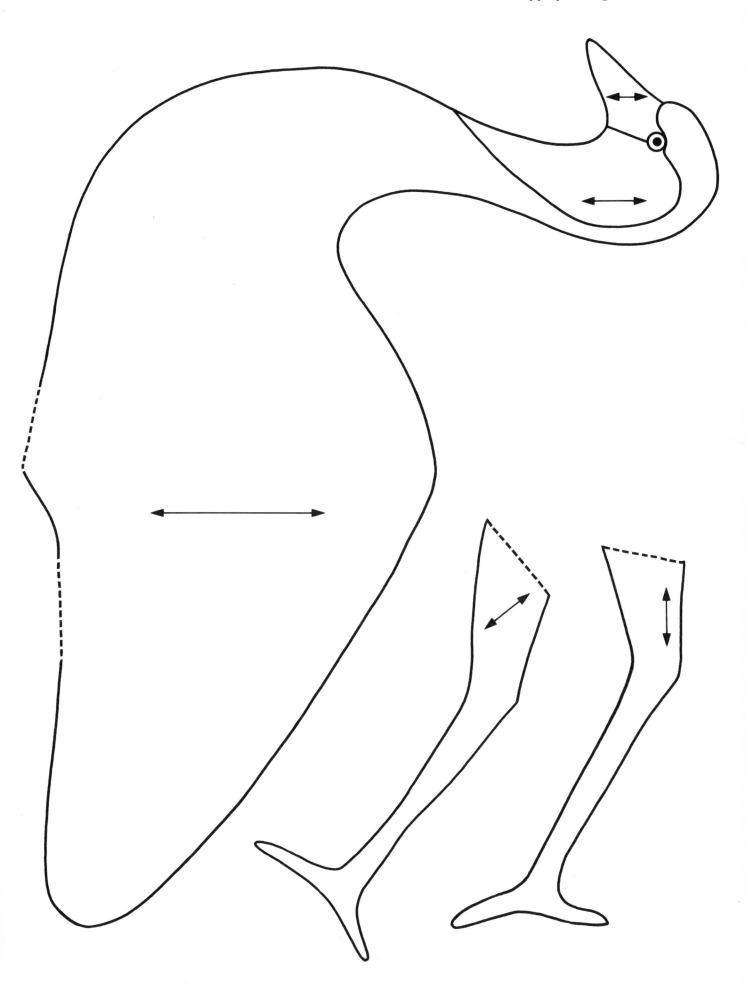

Eastern rosella

1 square = 3 cm (1¼″)

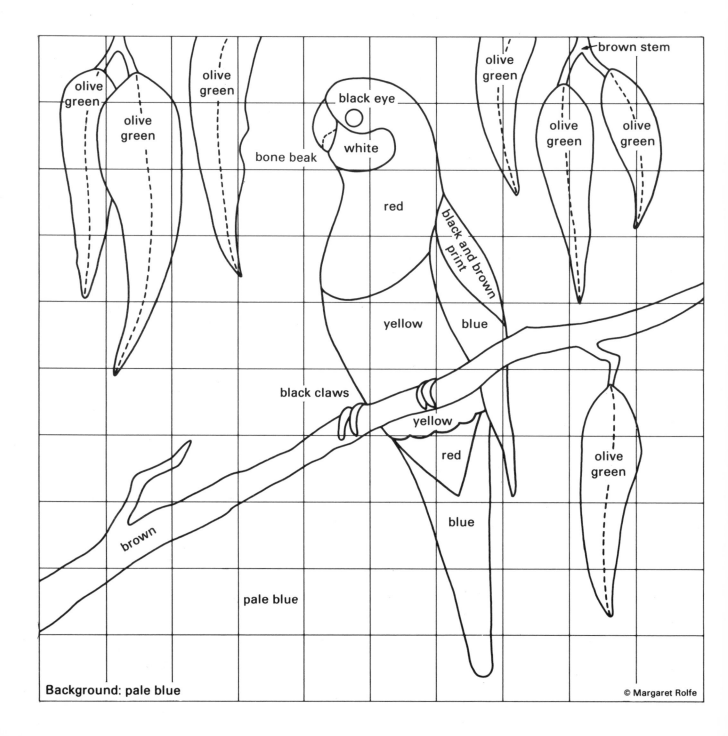

olive green · olive green · olive green · black eye · bone beak · white · olive green · brown stem · olive green · olive green · red · black and brown print · yellow · blue · black claws · yellow · red · olive green · brown · blue · pale blue

Background: pale blue

© Margaret Rolfe

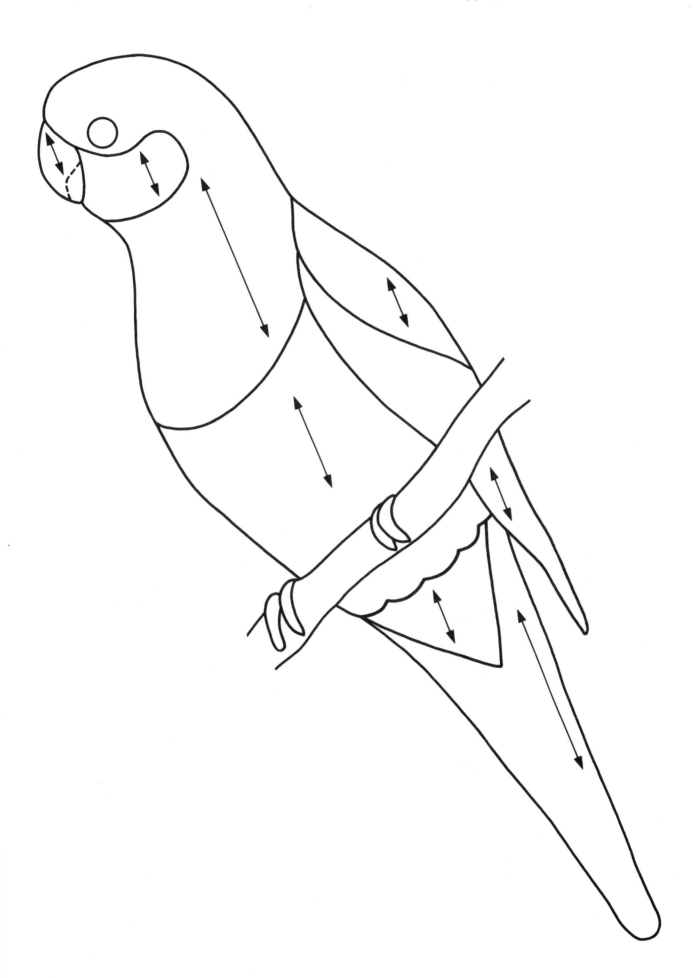

Kookaburra

1 square = 3 cm (1¼″)

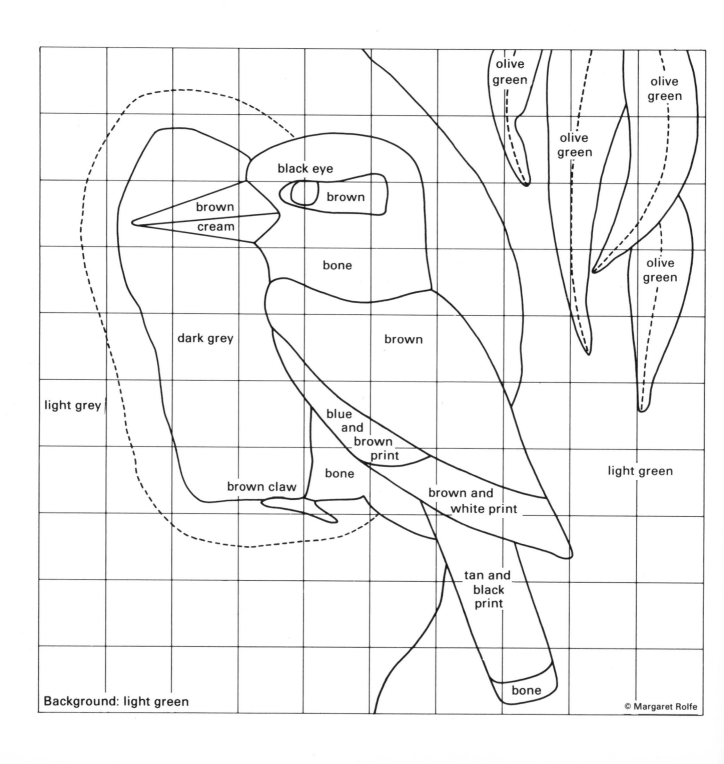

olive
green

olive
green

olive
green

black eye

brown

brown
cream

bone

olive
green

dark grey

brown

light grey

light green

blue
and
brown
print

bone

brown claw

bone

brown and
white print

tan and
black
print

bone

Background: light green

© Margaret Rolfe

Australian animals

Koala

1 square = 2 cm (¾″)

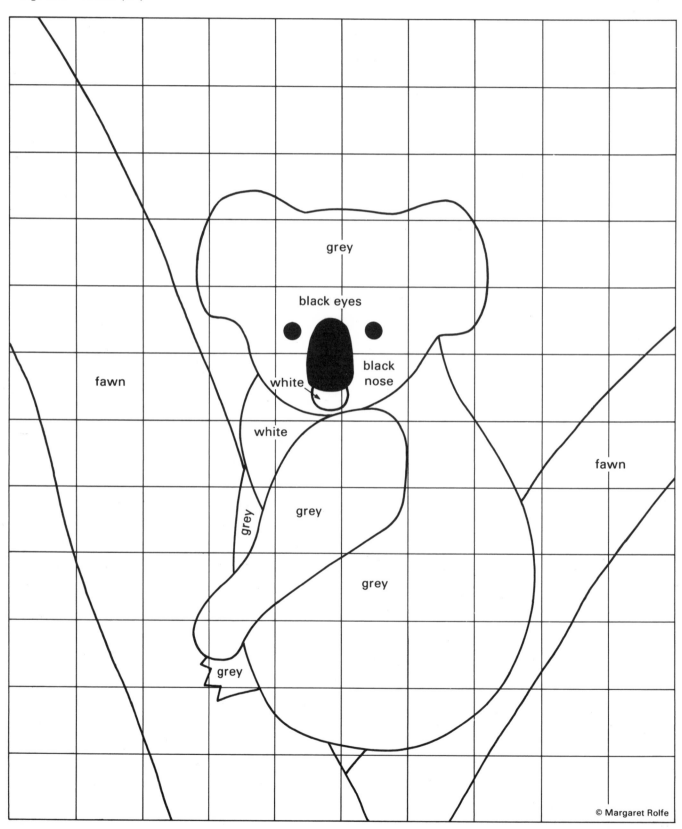

grey

black eyes

fawn

white

black
nose

white

fawn

grey

grey

grey

grey

Wombat

1 square = 2 cm (¾″)

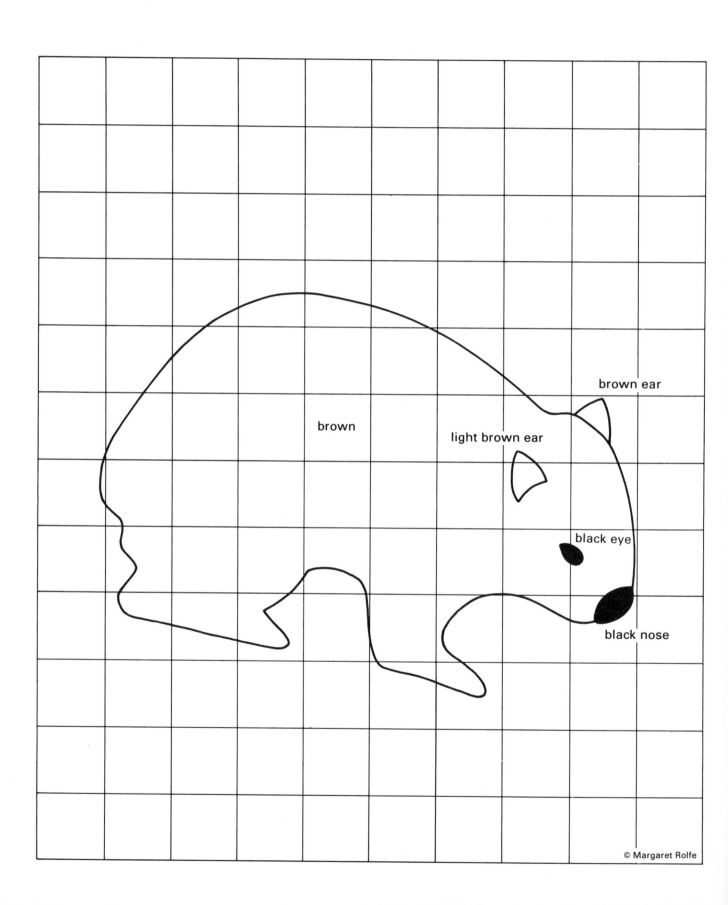

brown ear

brown

light brown ear

black eye

black nose

Echidna

1 square = 2 cm (¾″)

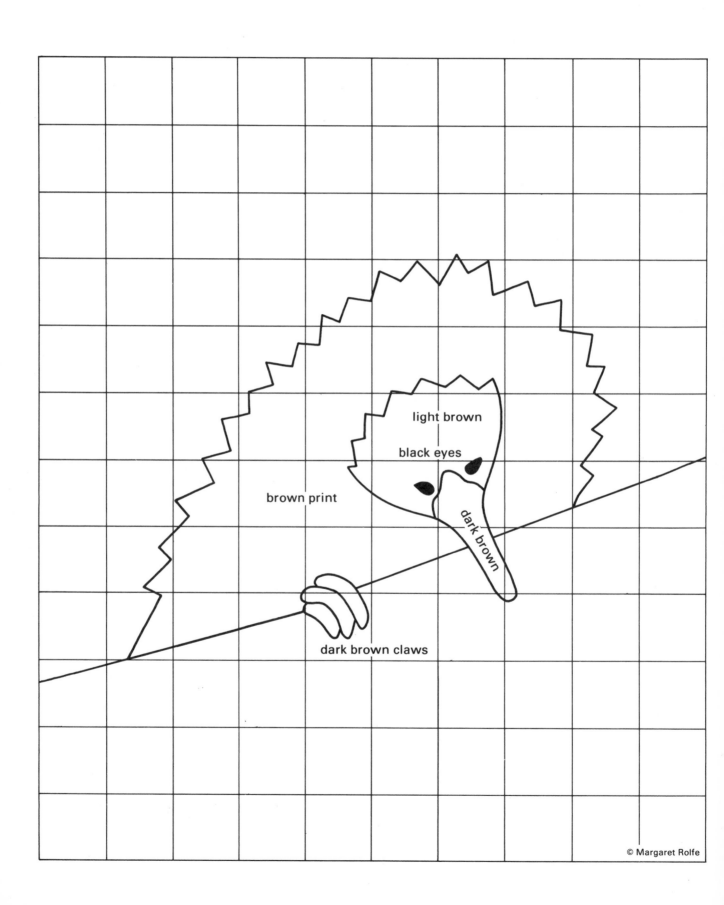

Kangaroo

1 square = 2 cm (¾″)

Facing: **Australian animals** *wallhanging by the author. The shy inhabitants of the Australian bush are the feature of this delightful wallhanging which was appliqued and quilted by hand. For applique animal designs, see page 80-91. For wallhanging construction, see page 144.*

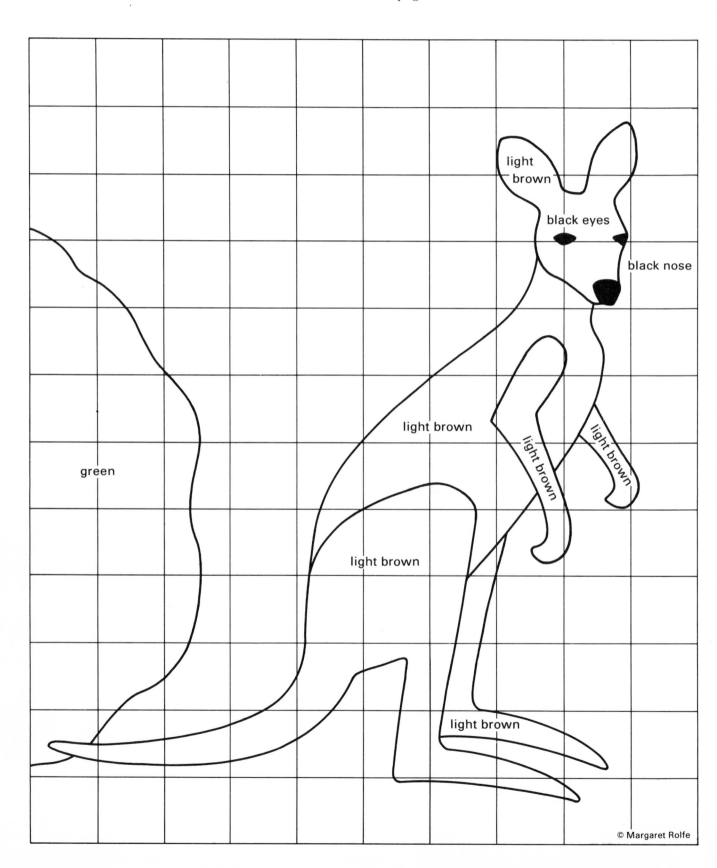

light brown

black eyes

black nose

light brown

light brown

light brown

green

light brown

light brown

light brown

© Margaret Rolfe

Facing: **Macrocarpa** *quilt by Marjorie Coleman.*
Australia's unique flora provides a rich source of
material for applique designs, such as this quilt inspired
by one of Western Australia's beautiful plants. Delicate
lines of hand quilting echo the shape of the plant.

Platypus

1 square = 2 cm (¾″)

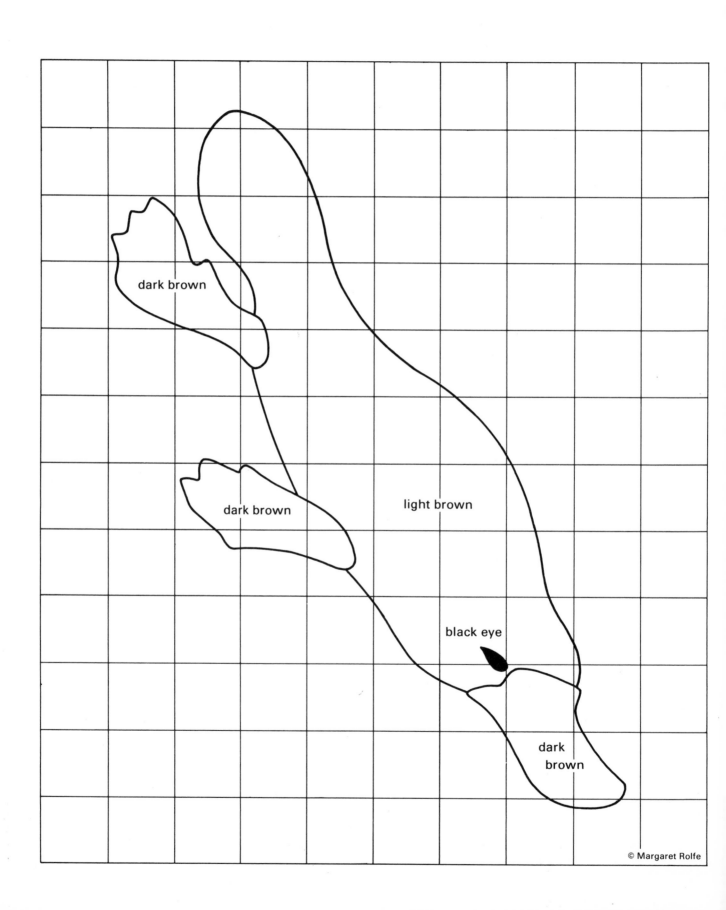

dark brown

dark brown

light brown

black eye

dark
brown

© Margaret Rolfe

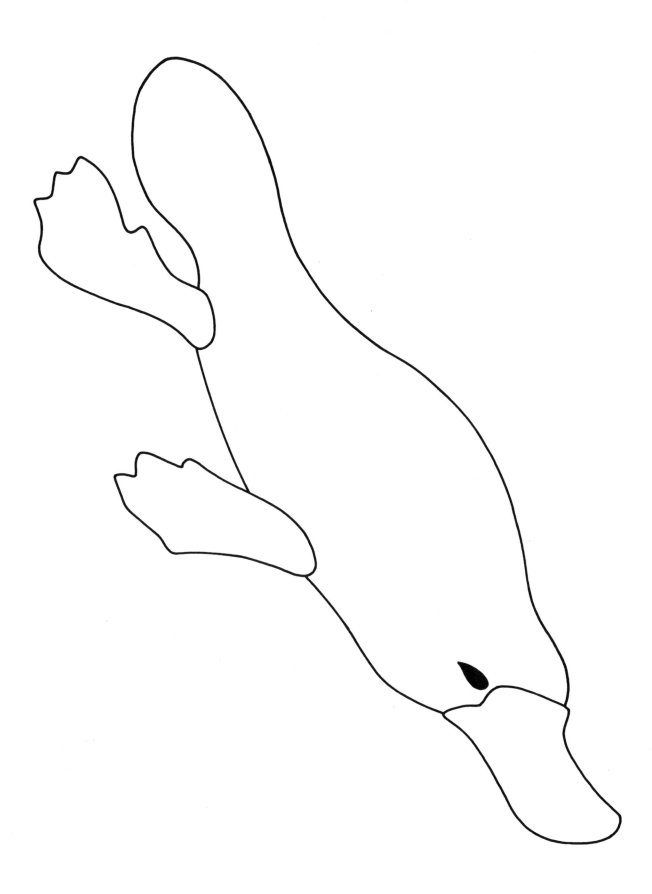

Possum

1 square = 2 cm (¾″)

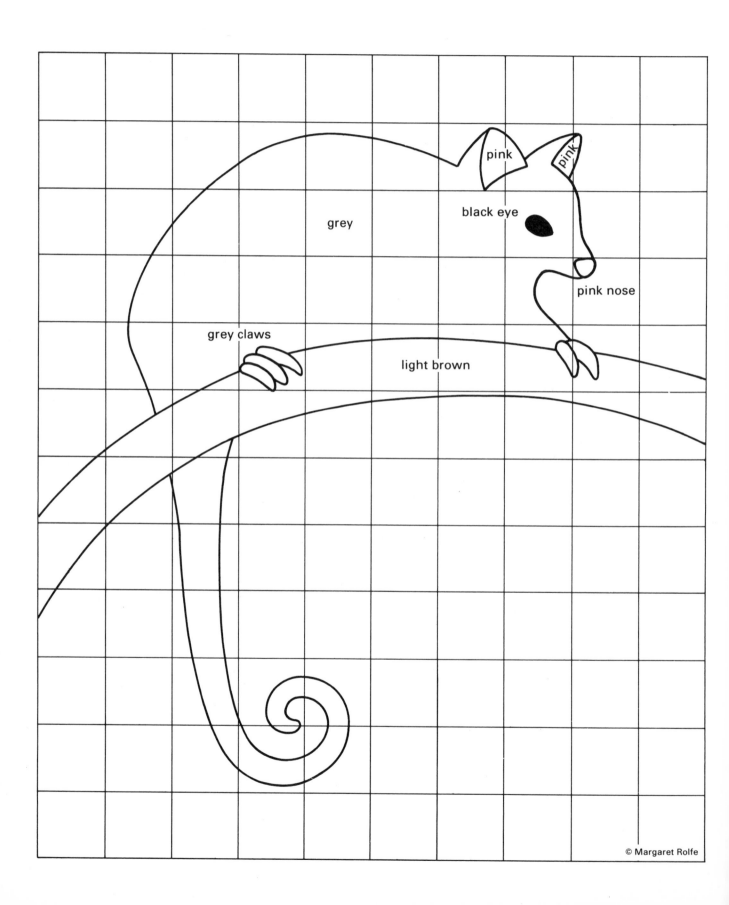

The labels within the figure read: grey, pink, pink, black eye, pink nose, grey claws, light brown.

Australian wildflowers

Waratah

1 square = 3 cm (1¼″)

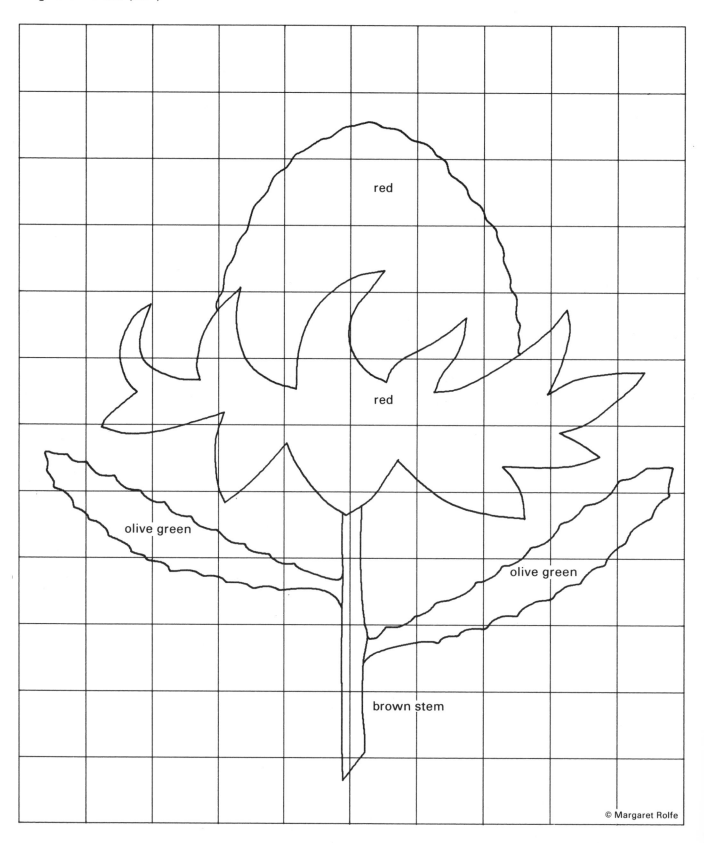

red

red

olive green

olive green

brown stem

© Margaret Rolfe

Golden wattle

1 square = 3 cm (1¼″)

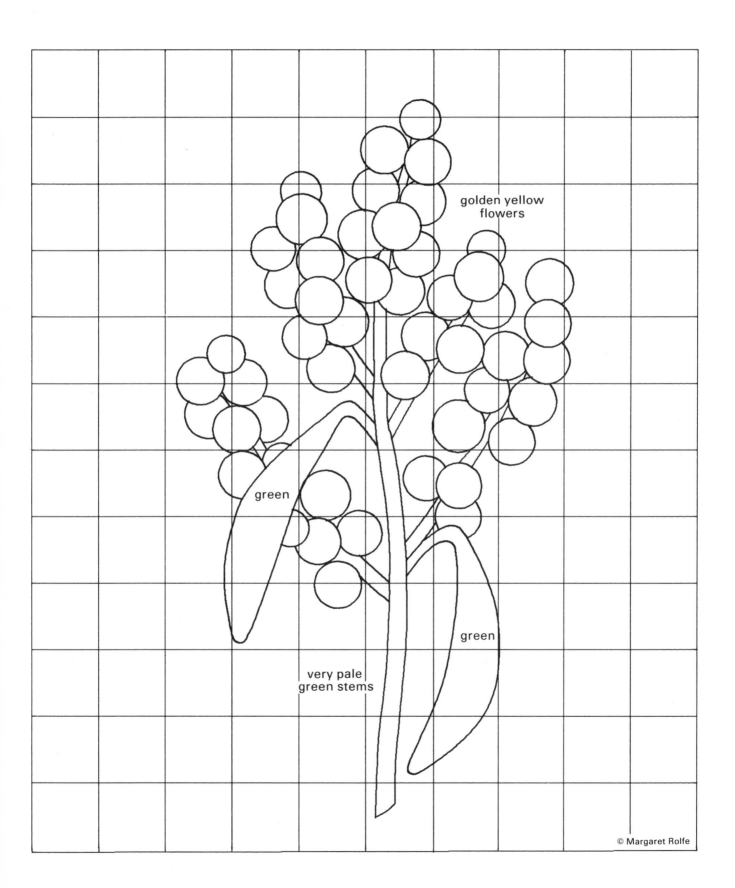

golden yellow
flowers

green

green

very pale
green stems

Red flowering gum

1 square = 3 cm (1¼″)

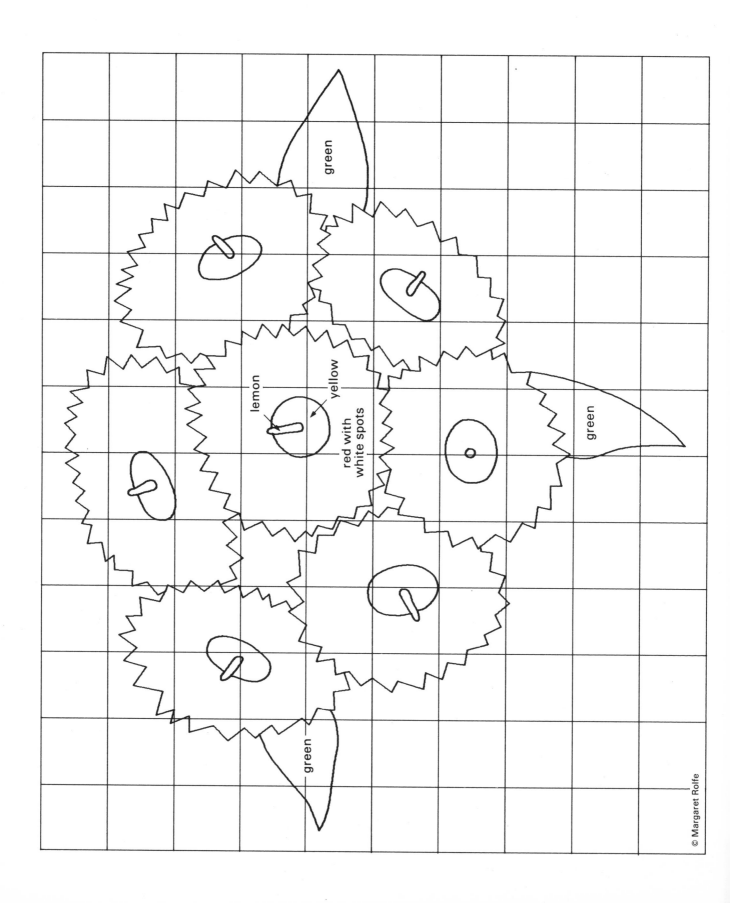

Cooktown orchid

1 square = 3 cm (1¼″)

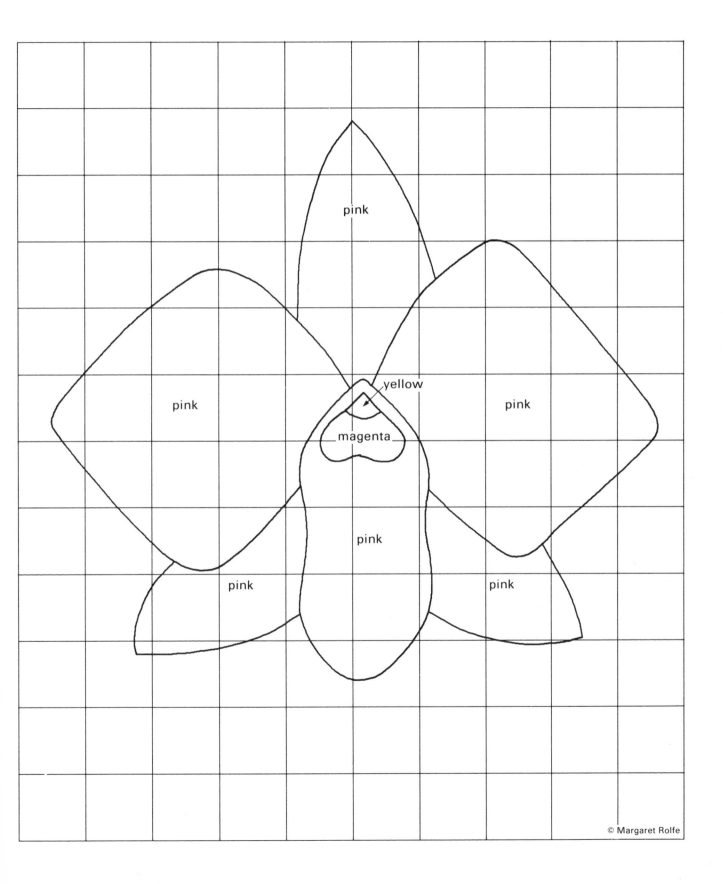

Giant waterlily

1 square = 3 cm (1¼")

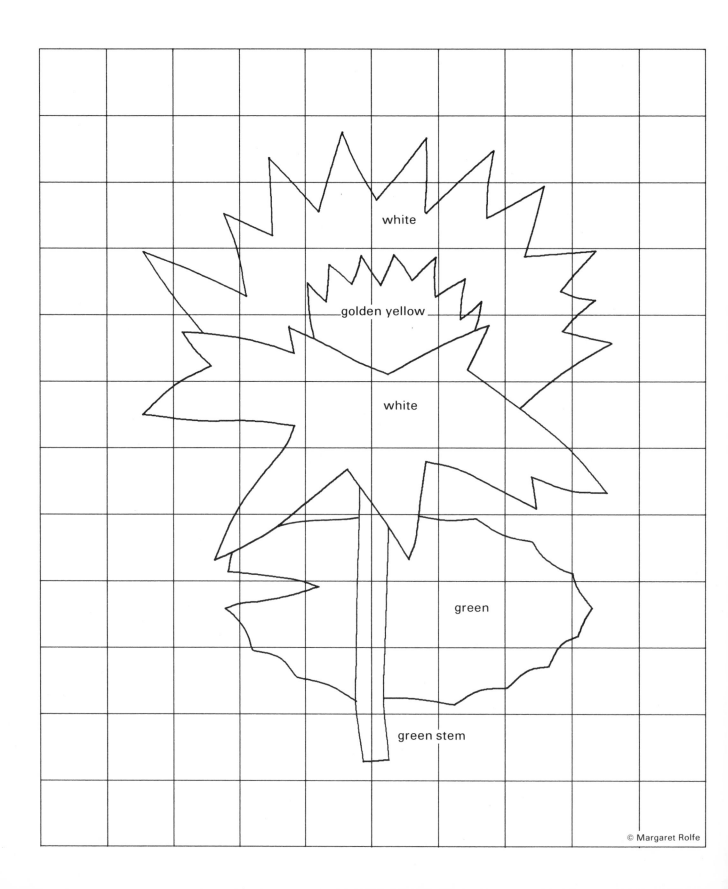

white

golden yellow

white

green

green stem

Everlasting daisy

1 square = 3 cm (1¼")

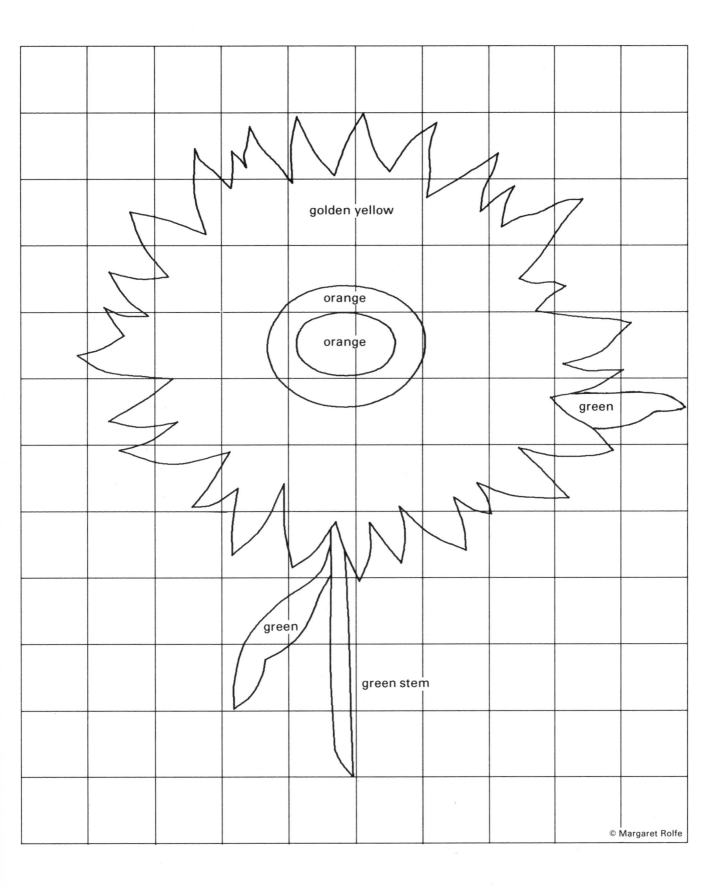

golden yellow

orange

orange

green

green

green stem

Sturt's desert pea

1 square = 3 cm (1¼″)

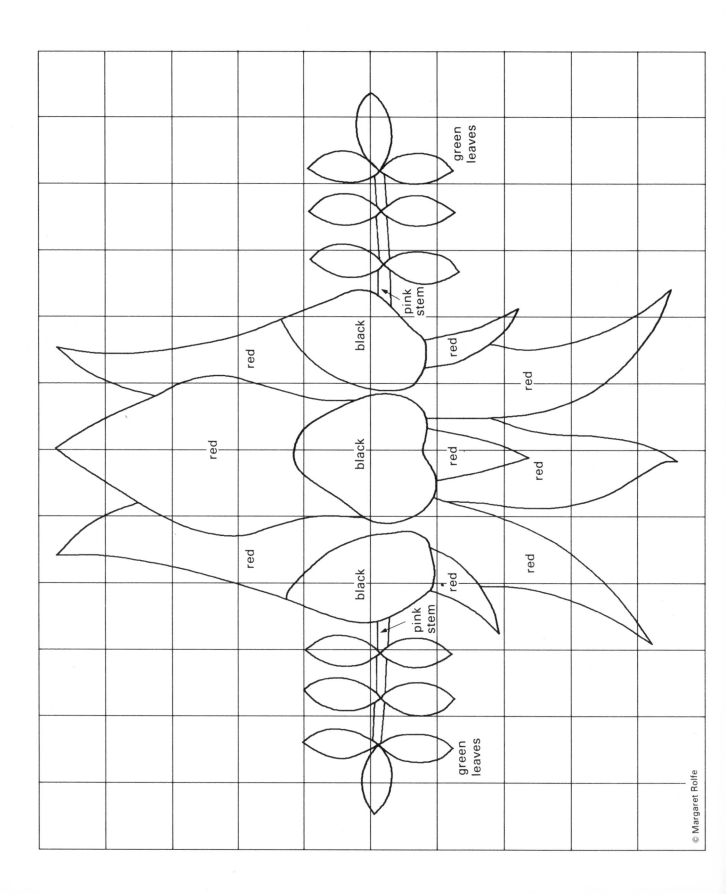

Guinea flower

1 square = 3 cm (1¼")

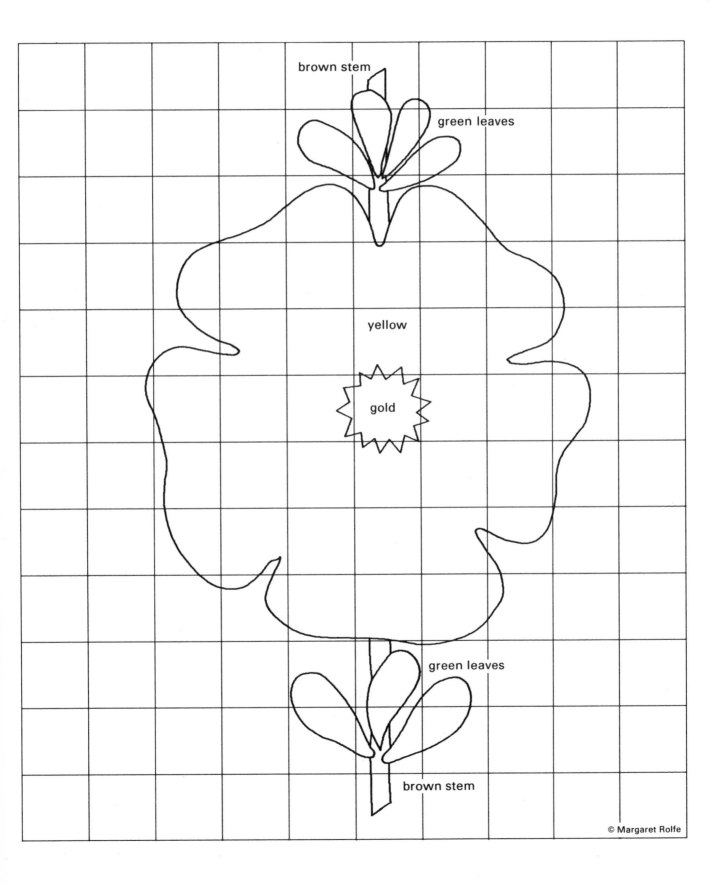

brown stem

green leaves

yellow

gold

green leaves

brown stem

Sturt's desert rose

1 square = 3 cm (1¼″)

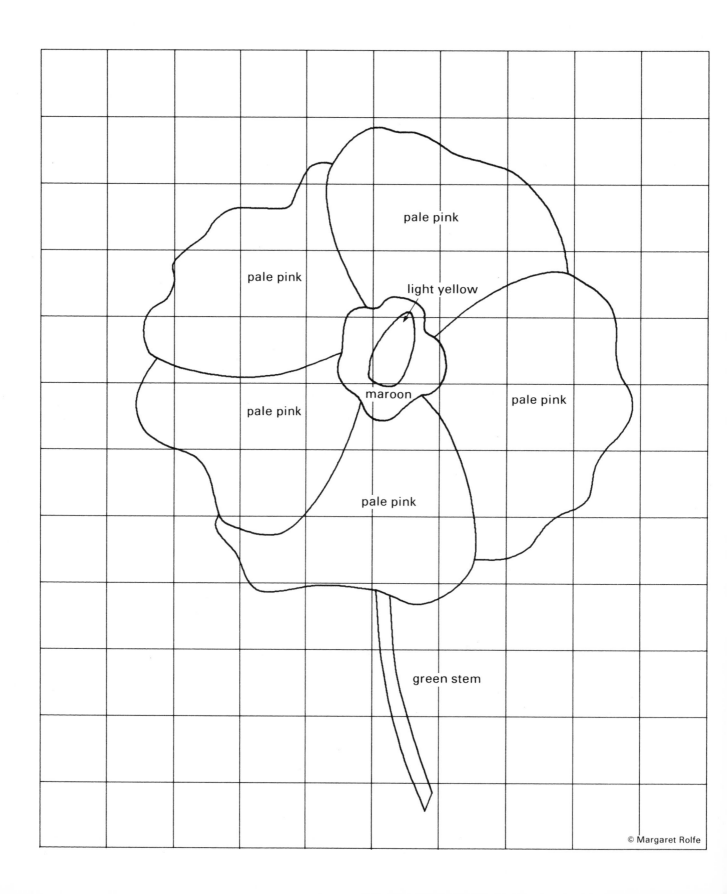

pale pink

pale pink

light yellow

pale pink

pale pink

maroon

pale pink

pale pink

green stem

© Margaret Rolfe

Pink heath

1 square = 3 cm (1¼″)

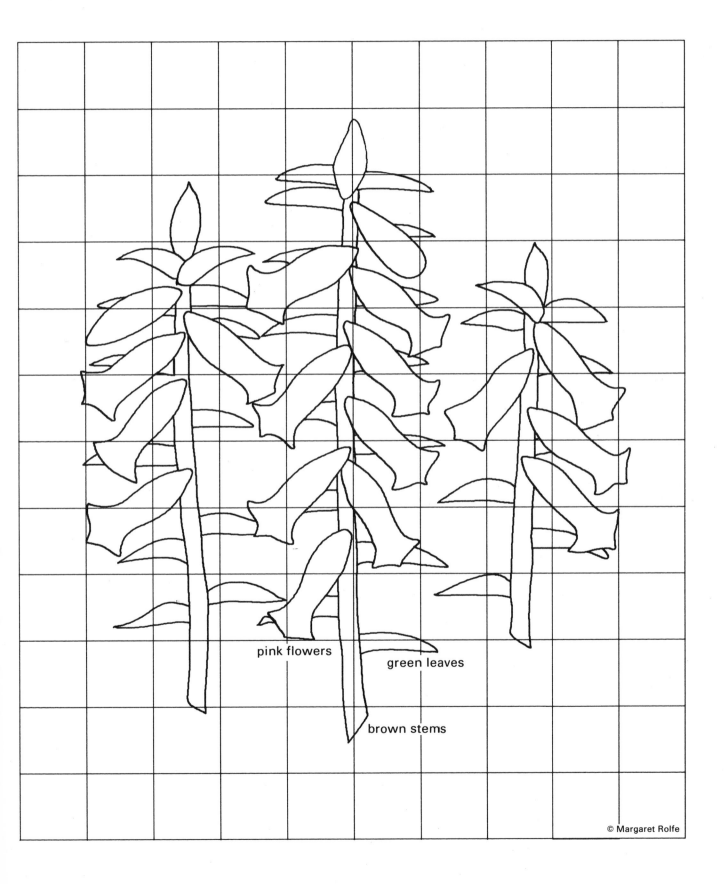

pink flowers

green leaves

brown stems

Purple flag

1 square = 3 cm (1¼″)

Facing: **Australian wildflowers** *quilt made by the author. The colour and variety of Australia's wild-flowers are represented in this quilt which was appliqued and quilted by hand. For applique flower designs, see pages 92-109. For wallhanging construction, see page 143.*

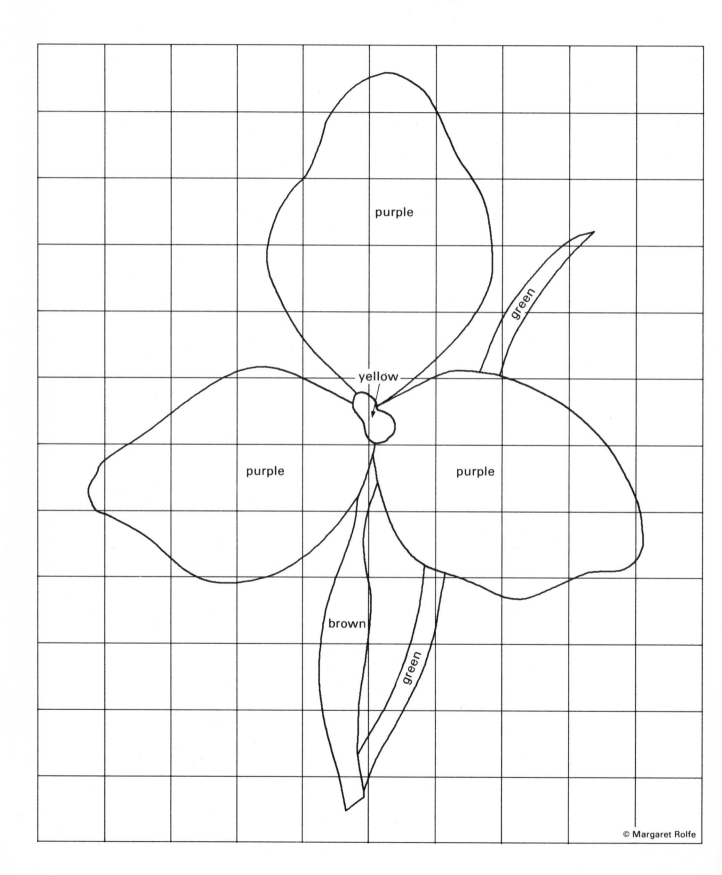

purple

green

yellow

purple

purple

brown

green

Flannel flower

1 square = 3 cm (1¼″)

Facing: **Fish, Turtle** *and* **Crab** *cushions made by the author. These vivid Aboriginal-style designs have been made using the bias applique technique. The cushions were machine quilted with lines following the appliqued shapes. For block designs see pages 112-4.*

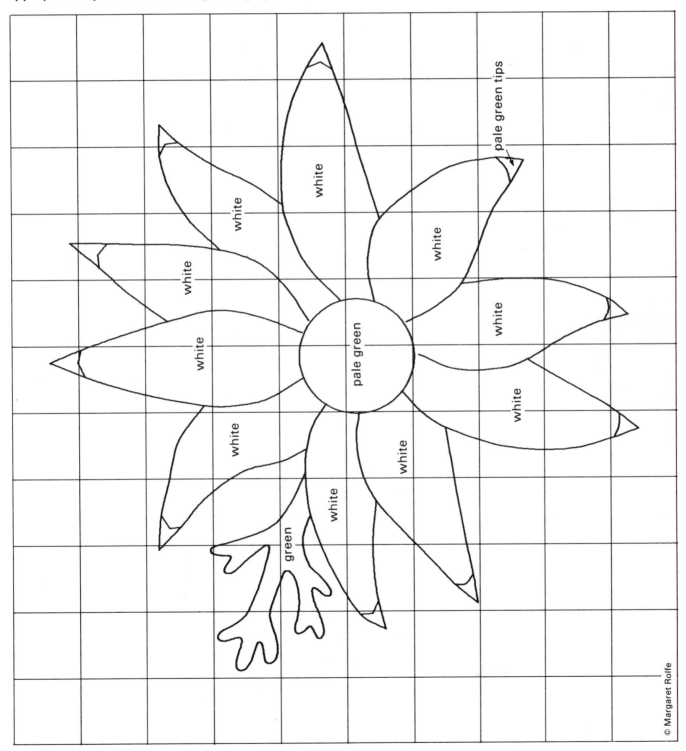

pale green tips

white

white

white

white

white

pale green

white

white

white

white

white

green

white

© Margaret Rolfe

Kangaroo paw

1 square = 3 cm (1¼″)

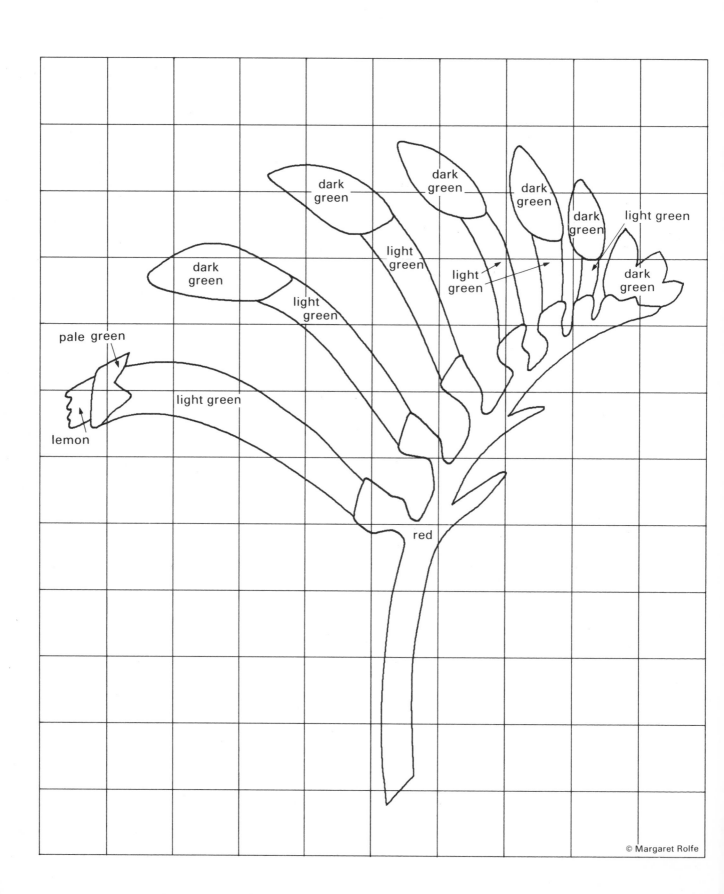

East-coast banksia

1 square = 3 cm (1¼″)

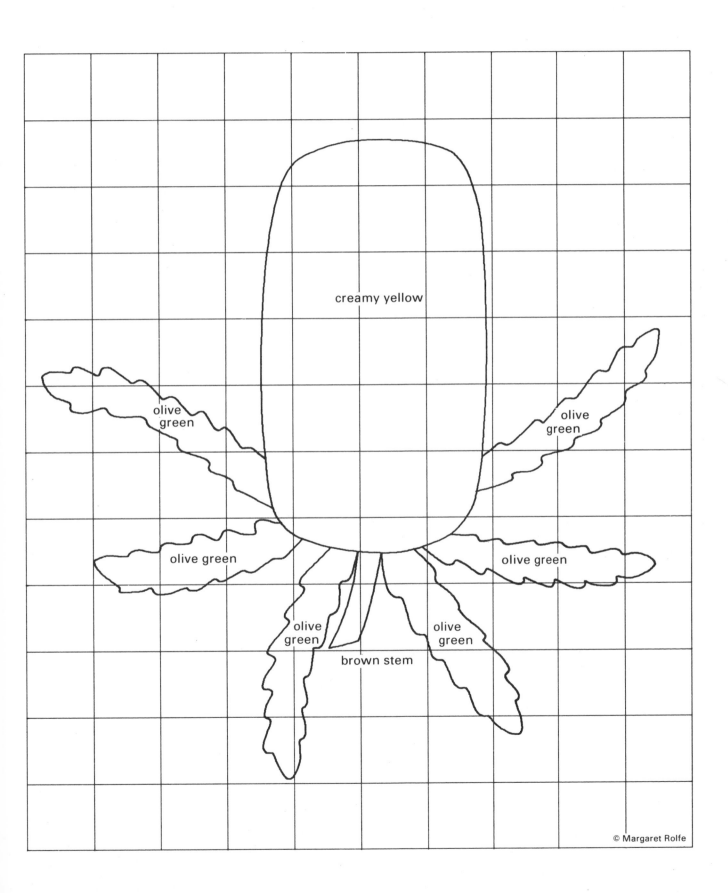

olive green

olive green

creamy yellow

olive green

olive green

olive green

olive green

brown stem

Tea-tree

1 square = 3 cm (1¼″)

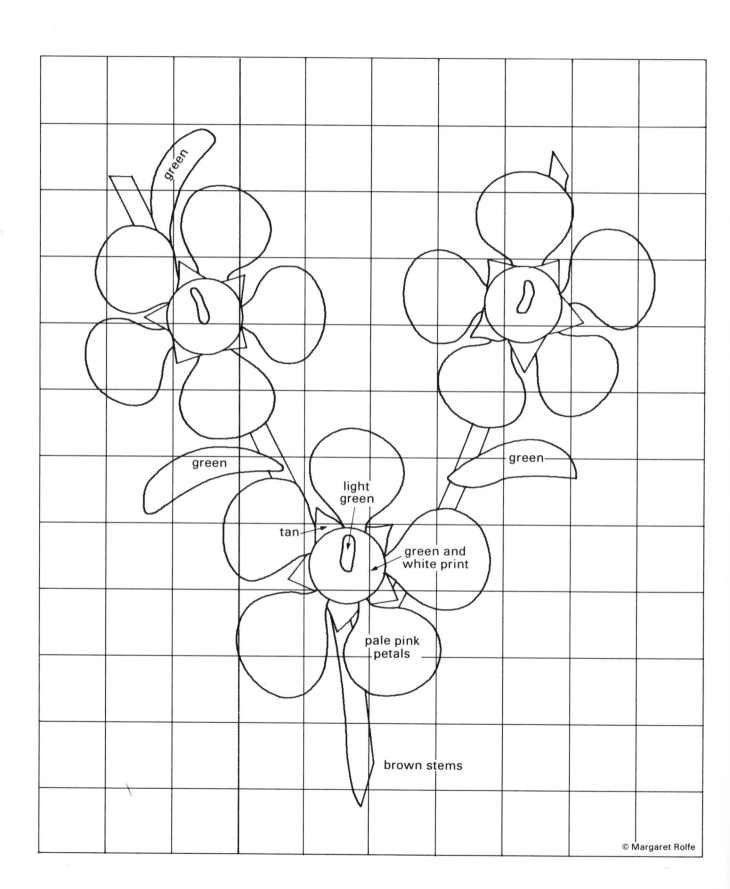

green

green

green

light
green

tan

green and
white print

pale pink
petals

brown stems

Crimson bottlebrush

l square = 3 cm (1¼")

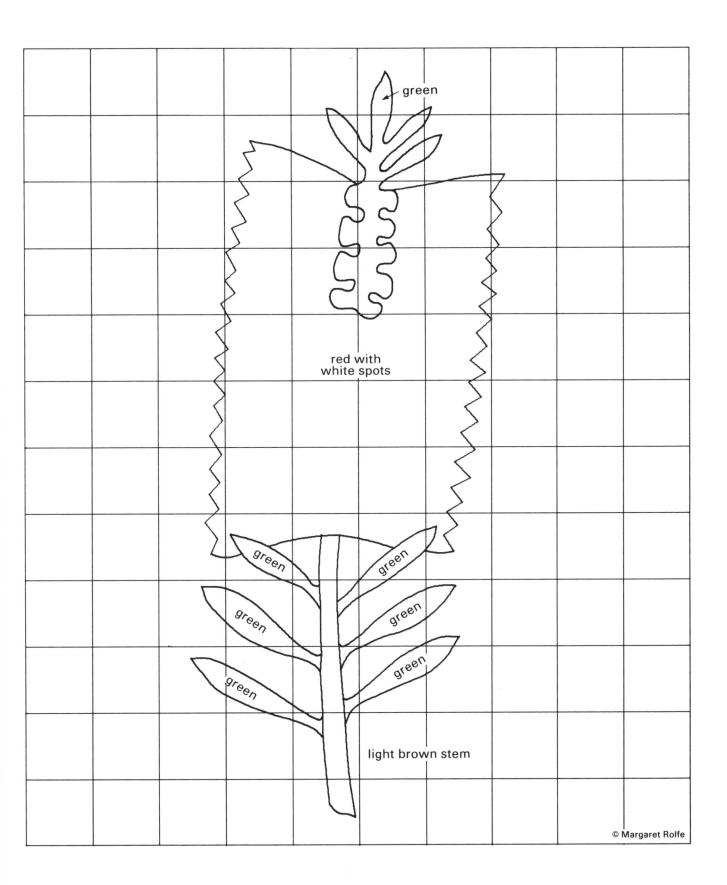

green

red with
white spots

green   green

green   green

green

light brown stem

Royal bluebell

1 square = 3 cm (1¼″)

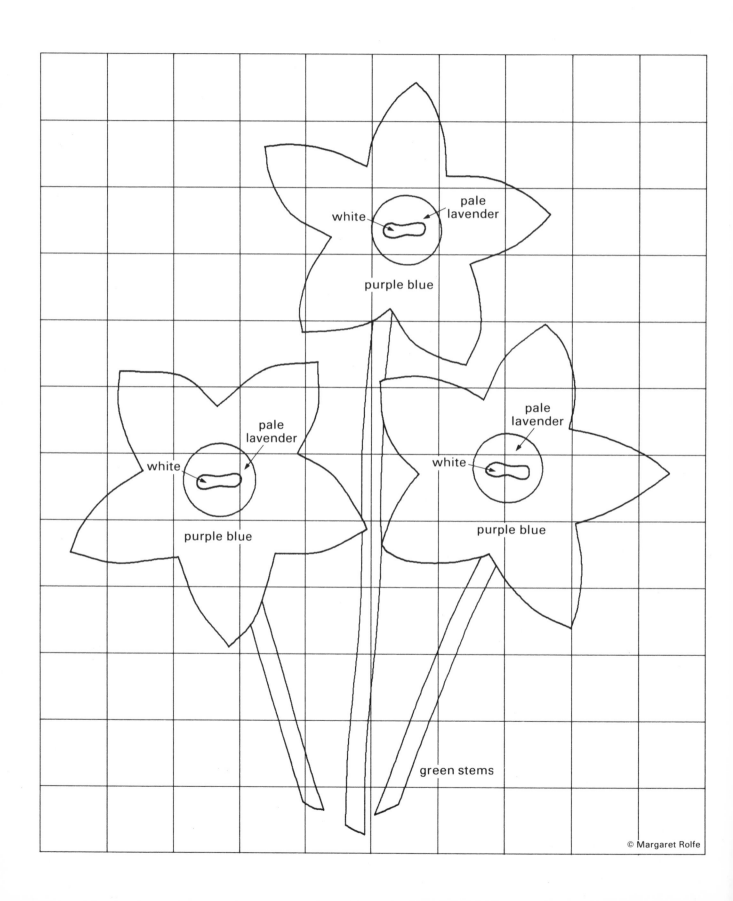

Christmas bells

l square = 3 cm (1¼″)

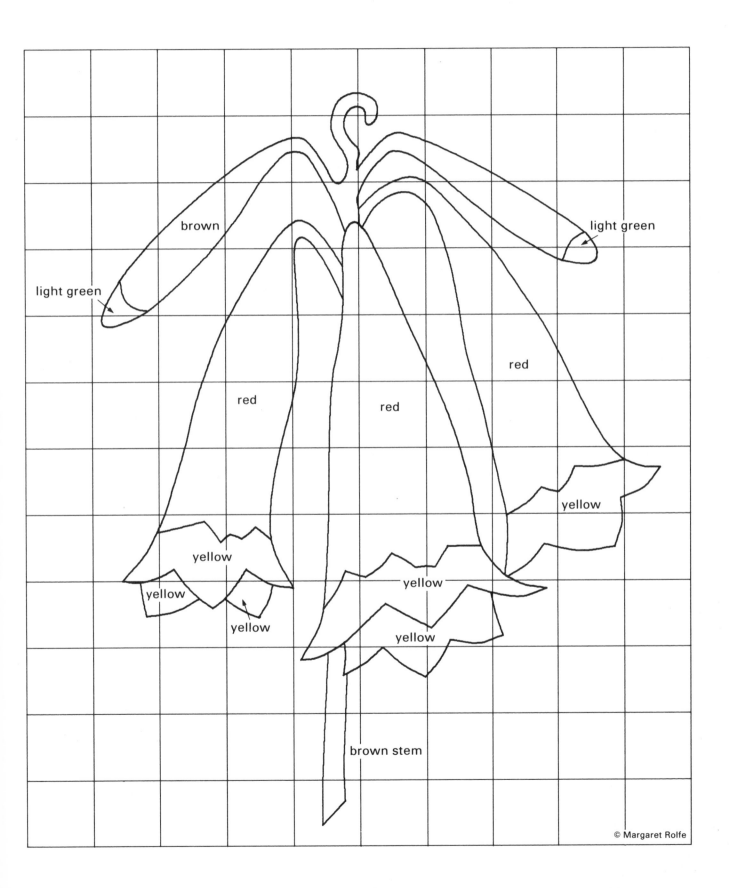

brown

light green

light green

red

red

red

yellow

yellow

yellow

yellow

yellow

brown stem

© Margaret Rolfe

Bias appliqué

Bias applique is where narrow strips of bias are used to cover the raw edges of the applique pieces. If the strips of bias are black, the technique gives the appearance of stained glass, and the technique is often referred to by this name. Pamela Tawton's **Flora Australiana** shows the stained-glass effect while, in my designs for **Turtle, Fish** and **Crab** cushions, bias applique is used to produce an effect reminiscent of the art of Australia's Aborigines.

Many of the same procedures that apply to ordinary applique also apply to bias applique. For instance, the grain of the materials should be matched wherever possible, to ensure that the applique will lie flat.

Designing for bias appliqué

One of the main considerations when designing for bias applique is to avoid having pieces which are too small for the bias to curve around. Look for designs with smooth lines and gentle curves. A stained glass effect can be further enhanced by using several shades of one colour as a background.

The bias strips

The bias strips should be made from a soft material which will take the curves easily. I suggest using a good quality cotton lawn. Cut the strips, on the true bias, 2 cm (¾″) wide. To help with this, you may like to make yourself a template by cutting a firm piece of cardboard into a long 2 cm-wide (¾″) strip. Use this strip either to mark your fabric before cutting, or when cutting with a rotary cutter. Purchased bias binding is really not satisfactory to use, as it is too wide and some is not of good enough quality.

Prepare your bias strips by folding them lengthways into thirds (but don't let the cut edge show on the top), and then tacking (basting) down the centre of each folded strip.

How to bias appliqué

Step 1
Enlarge and copy the design. Using graph paper or a large piece of paper, make a grid of squares the required size. Draw your design in pencil, and when you are happy with it, go over it with a black pen. Number each part of the design in a systematic way to help you locate the position of the pieces later. This becomes your master copy.

Step 2
Using a sheet of tracing paper, and holding the layers together with paper clips, trace the design from the master copy. Mark each piece with a grain line—the lines of your grid will help you. Go over the tracing with black pen.

Step 3
Prepare a backing fabric. To achieve a stained-glass effect, you will completely cover this backing, so it can be a piece of plain material such as white lawn. To help you position all your pieces correctly, transfer the pattern onto the backing. Do this by taping your tracing onto a window or light box, taping your backing fabric over it, then copying the design onto the backing with a pencil.

For other bias applique, such as the Aboriginal style designs, you can use a *background* fabric for the backing. This background fabric will not be completely covered up, so it is not necessary to trace the design onto it, and of course it will be of the colour that you have chosen for the background.

Step 4
Cut out each applique piece from the tracing paper.

Step 5
Pin your tracing paper patterns to the different fabric needed for each of the applique pieces, remembering to match the grain with the grain marked on your pattern. Cut out the

pieces, allowing 2 mm (¹⁄₁₆″) around each piece, so that they will all overlap slightly when put together.

Step 6
Assemble all the pieces onto the backing or background fabric, putting the pieces in their appropriate places and matching the grain of the pieces to the background. Pin in place, and tack (baste).

Step 7
If you are going to applique the bias strips by hand, each piece needs to be firmly anchored in place with a running stitch around the edge, stitching only 2 mm (¹⁄₁₆″) from the cut edge (this stitching will be hidden under the bias). Running stitching is not necessary if you will be stitching on the bias using a machine.

Step 8
Prepare your strips of bias as described earlier.

Step 9
If you are *hand sewing* the bias, pin the bias strips over the raw edges of the applique, working on one section at a time. The thing to watch for in this instance is that the end of all your strips are neatly tucked under the over-lapping pieces. It is very annoying to stitch down a length of bias, only to discover later that the end of another should have been stitched under it! It is prudent to leave the ends dangling until you have worked out how they will finish, then cut and stitch them later. Pin the bias carefully before you sew it down, especially around the curves. It helps keep the bias smooth if you always pin around the *inside* of the curve, since the bias always stretches around the outside of curves. Because bias will stretch, but not compress, it will bunch up on the inside of the curves if you pin the outside of the curves first. Fold the bias neatly around sharp corners.

If you are *machine sewing* the bias, first tack (baste) all the bias in place, planning carefully how the raw ends will be tucked in and hidden. When you are tacking around a curve, tack the *inside* of the curve, so that the bias will stretch smoothly (it will look as if it wants to sit up at an angle, but it *will* stitch flat under the machine).

Step 10
Stitch the bias down. If you are *hand sewing*, use the almost invisible stitch used in applique —coming up through the backing and applique piece and into the fold of the bias . . . stitching straight down again . . . coming back up through all layers a little further on, and so on. Use thread to match the bias and stitch both sides of the bias strips, remembering to sew the inside (concave) curves first.

If you are *machine sewing*, again use a thread to match the bias strips, and stitch slowly and carefully just inside the edge of both sides of the bias strips. Begin and end with several back stitches.

Bias appliqué designs

Aboriginal~style designs

Turtle

1 square = 3 cm (1¼″)

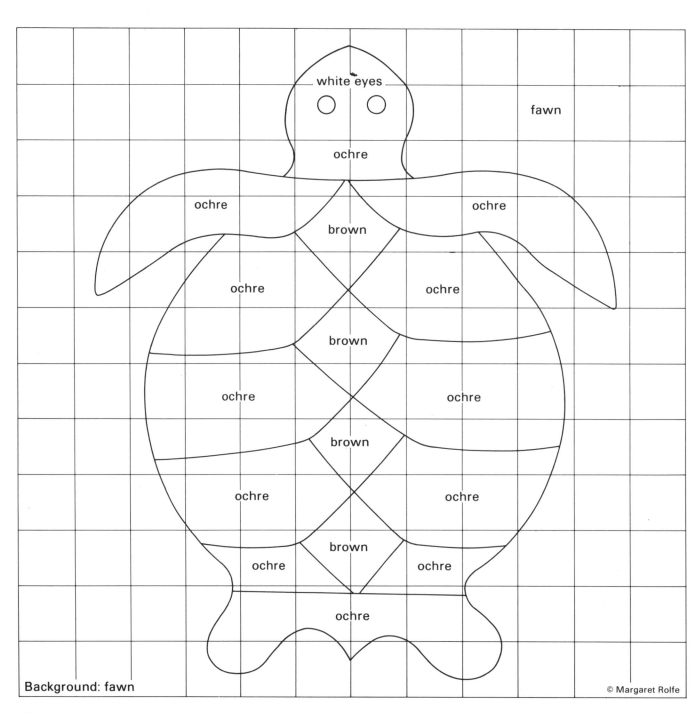

white eyes

fawn

ochre

ochre

ochre

brown

ochre

ochre

brown

ochre

ochre

brown

ochre

ochre

brown

ochre

ochre

ochre

Background: fawn

© Margaret Rolfe

Fish

1 square = 3 cm (1¼")

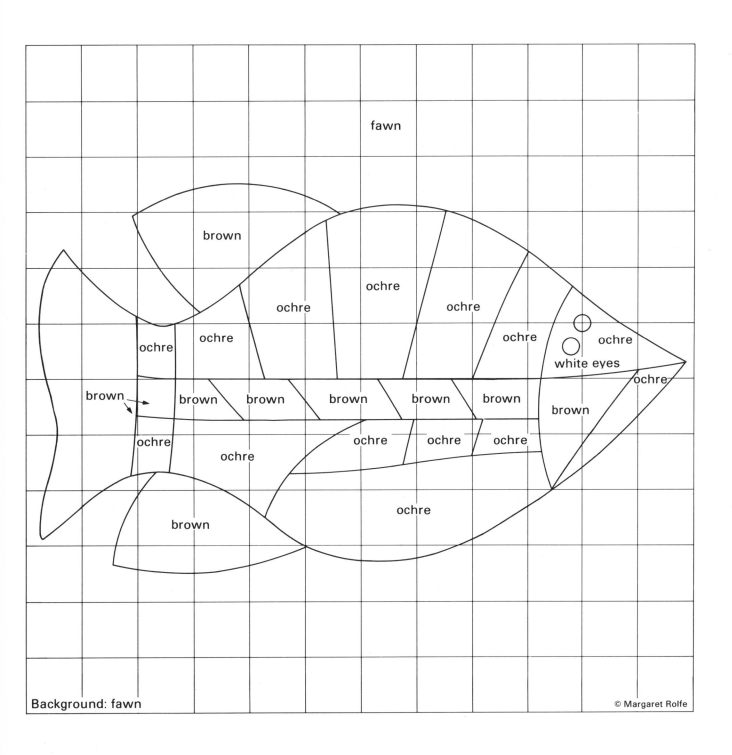

Background: fawn

Crab

l square = 4 cm (1½″)

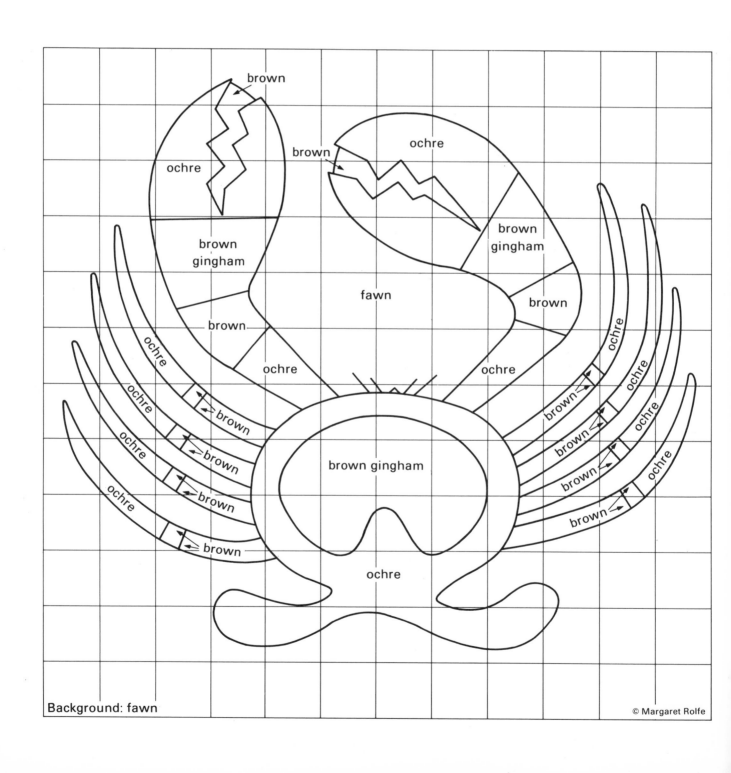

Flora Australiana designs

Designed by Pamela Tawton

Christmas bells

1 square = 35 mm (1½″)

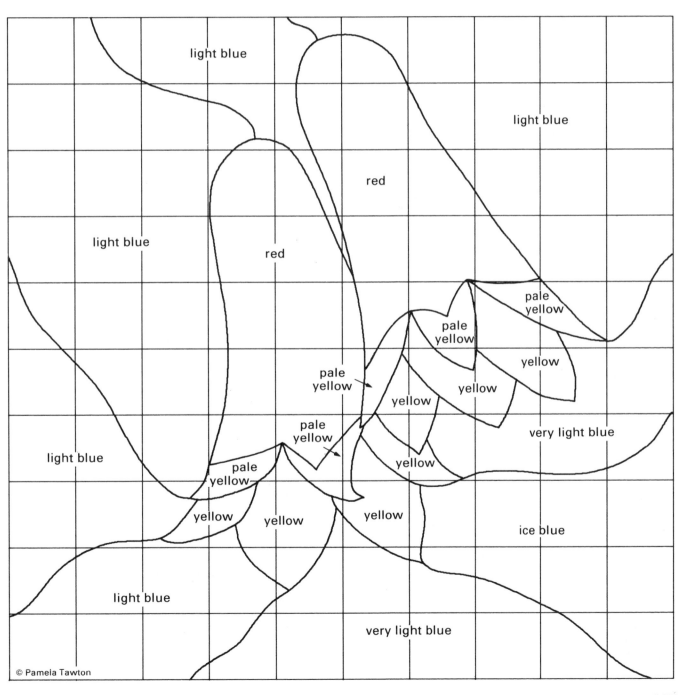

light blue

light blue

red

light blue

red

pale
yellow

pale
yellow

yellow

pale
yellow

yellow

yellow

very light blue

light blue

pale
yellow

pale
yellow

yellow

yellow

yellow

yellow

ice blue

light blue

very light blue

Sturt's desert rose

1 square = 35 mm (1½″)

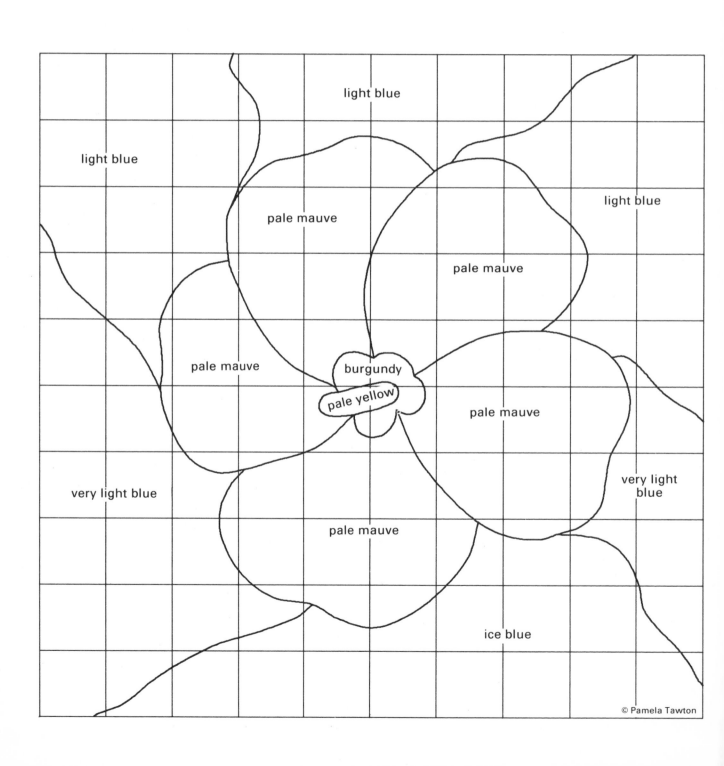

light blue

light blue

light blue

pale mauve

pale mauve

pale mauve

burgundy

pale yellow

pale mauve

very light blue

very light
blue

pale mauve

ice blue

The egg and bacon pea

1 square = 35 mm (1½″)

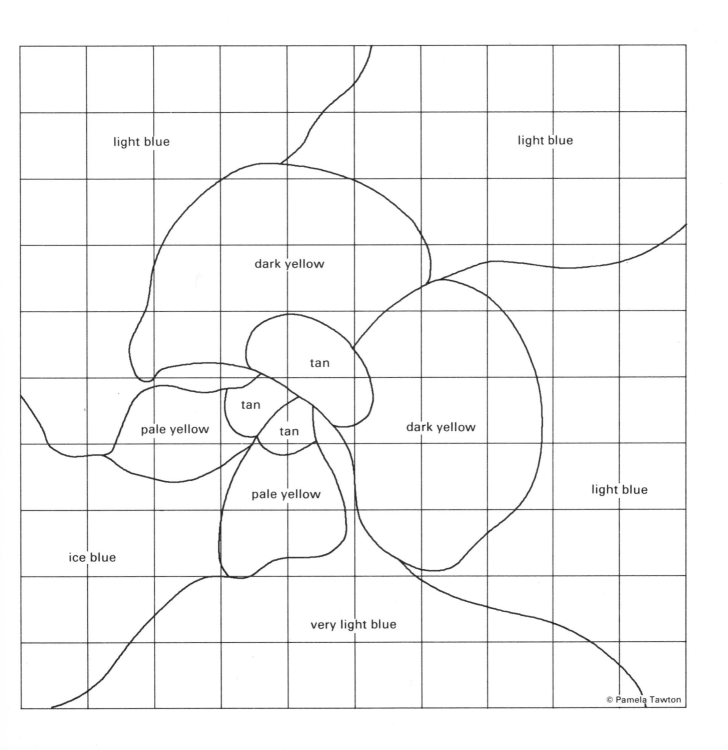

light blue

light blue

dark yellow

tan

tan

pale yellow

tan

dark yellow

light blue

pale yellow

ice blue

very light blue

© Pamela Tawton

Purple flag iris

1 square = 35 mm (1½″)

Facing: **Flora Australiana** *wallhanging made by Pamela Tawton. The stained-glass style of bias applique was used to create this dramatic hand-appliqued wallhanging of nine Australian wildflowers. For applique wildflower designs, see pages 115-23. For wallhanging construction, see page 145.*

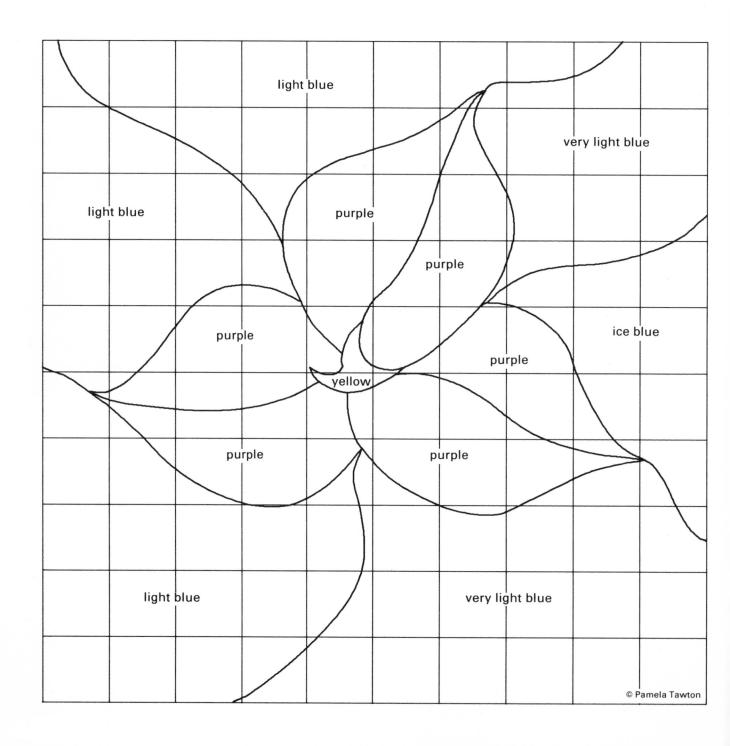

light blue

very light blue

light blue

purple

purple

ice blue

purple

purple

yellow

purple

purple

purple

light blue

very light blue

© Pamela Tawton

Step-by-step: Bias appliqué—stained-glass style

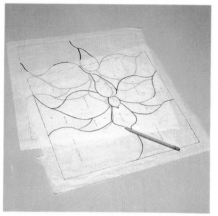

Step 1   Draw design full size onto paper, copy onto tracing paper and cut out. Cut out fabric pieces from tracing paper patterns, adding 2 mm (1⁄16″) all around.

Step 2   Prepare bias strips by cutting strips of fabric, on the bias, 2 cm (3⁄4″) wide. Fold strips in three, and tack along the centre.

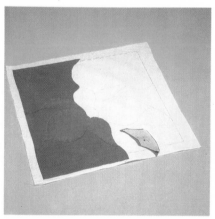

Step 3   Trace design onto background fabric. Pin and tack pieces in place. Sew a row of running stitches around outside of each piece.

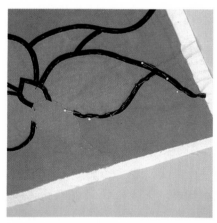

Step 4   Pin bias in place, pinning concave side around curves so bias will stretch neatly without puckering. Plan carefully where bias strips will overlap and end.

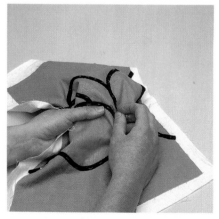

Step 5   Stitch bias in place, using a thread that matches the bias strips.

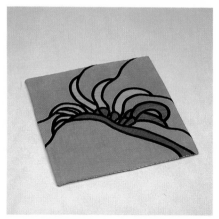

Step 6   A finished bias applique block, showing the **Kangaroo paw** design.

Sturt's desert pea

1 square = 35 mm (1½″)

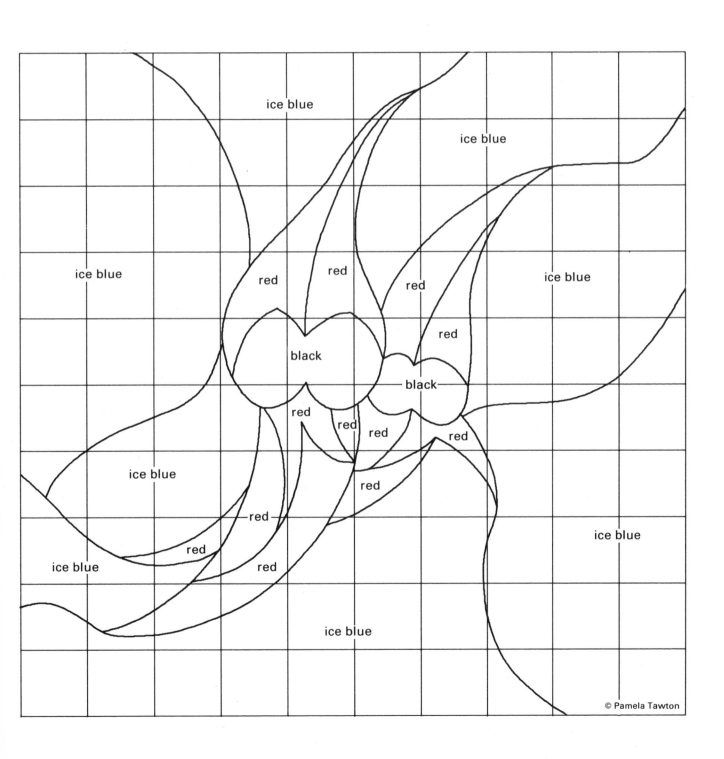

ice blue

ice blue

ice blue

red

red

red

red

ice blue

black

red

black

red

red
red

red

red

ice blue

red

red

red

ice blue

ice blue

ice blue

Royal bluebell

1 square = 35 mm (1½″)

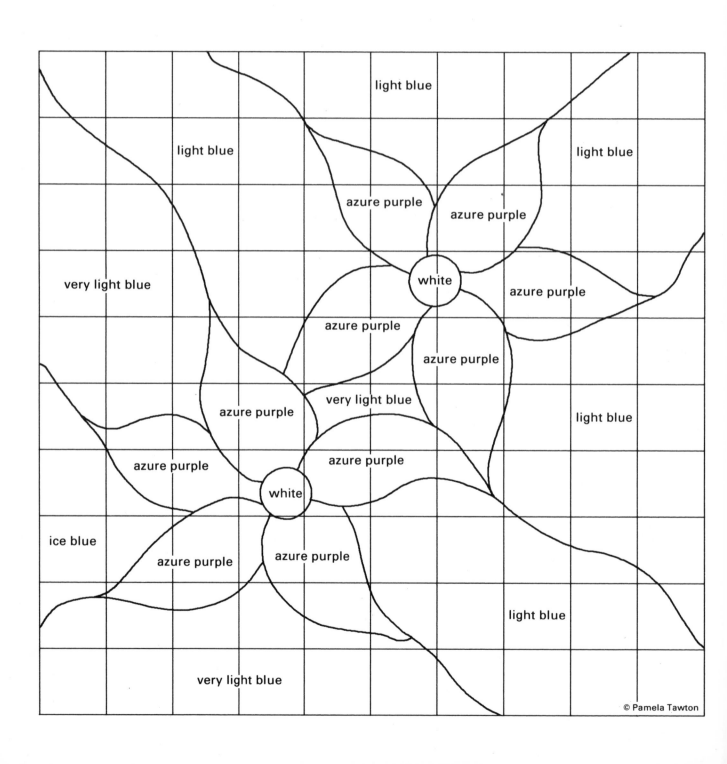

light blue

light blue

light blue

azure purple

azure purple

azure purple

very light blue

white

azure purple

azure purple

azure purple

very light blue

light blue

azure purple

azure purple

azure purple

white

ice blue

azure purple

azure purple

light blue

very light blue

© Pamela Tawton

Flannel flower

1 square = 35 mm (1½″)

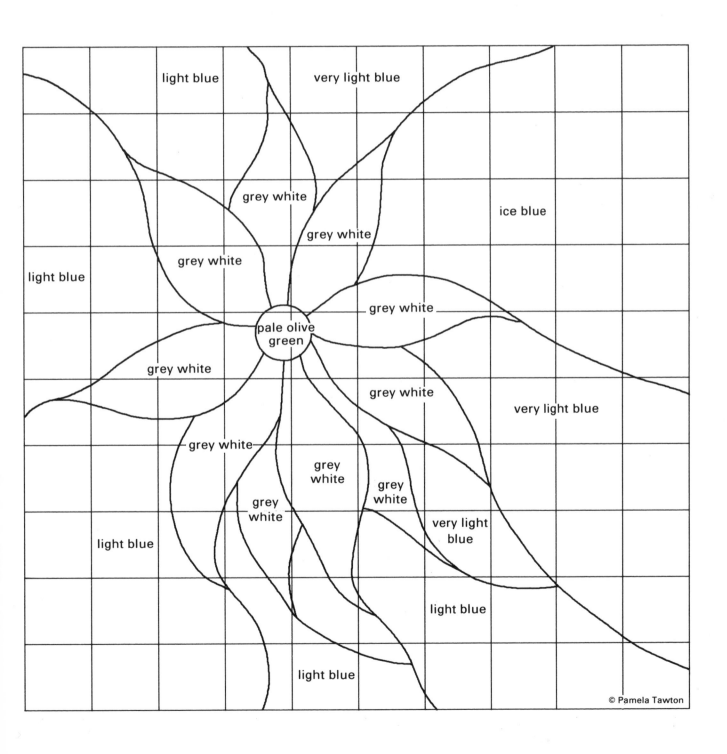

light blue

very light blue

grey white

grey white

ice blue

grey white

light blue

grey white

grey white

pale olive green

grey white

grey white

grey white

very light blue

grey white

grey white

grey white

very light blue

light blue

light blue

light blue

© Pamela Tawton

Cooktown orchid

1 square = 35 mm (1½″)

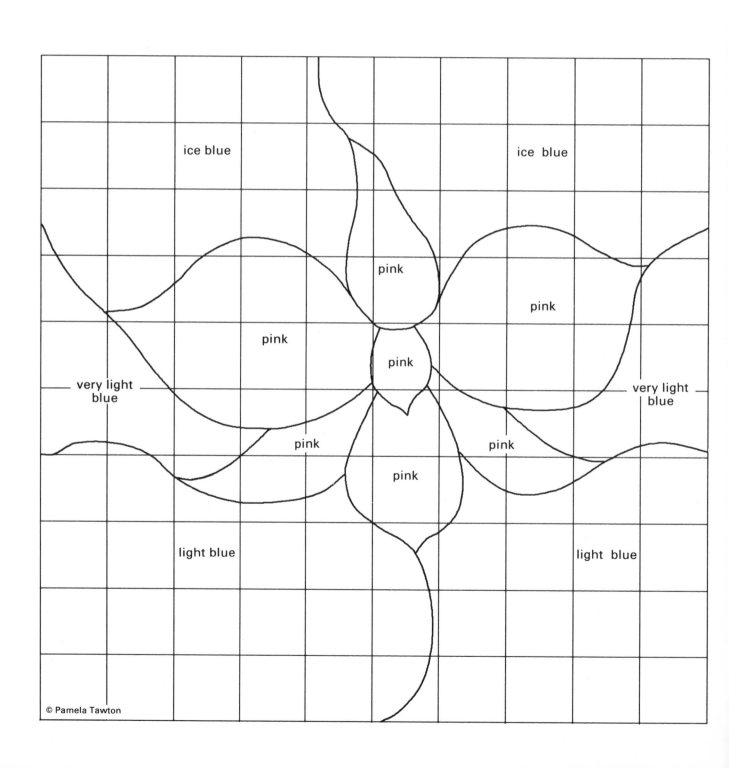

ice blue

ice blue

pink

pink

pink

pink

very light
blue

very light
blue

pink

pink

pink

light blue

light blue

Kangaroo paw

l square = 35 mm (1½″)

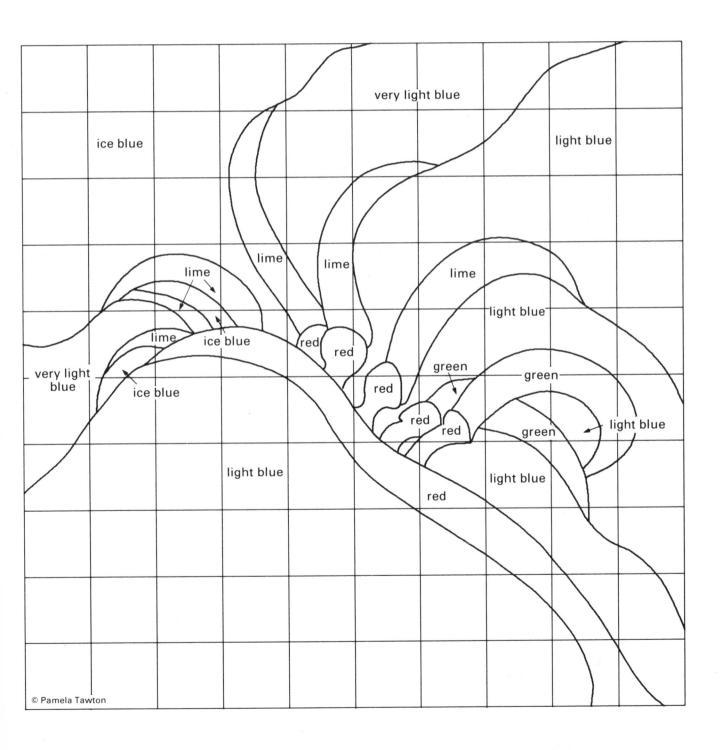

© Pamela Tawton

Quilting by hand

Hand quilting is just a simple running stitch that joins the three layers of the quilt 'sandwich' together. However, some special equipment is necessary for hand quilting. A short needle called a *between* is always used, and these come in a variety of thicknesses. You will also find a thimble is essential to protect your finger.

Quilting thread is used for the stitching, as it is stronger than normal sewing thread.

Quilting involving small pieces can be done in your lap. Alternatively, a hoop or frame can be used for both small or large pieces. Some people prefer to make quilts in small sections which they quilt and join later—this is sometimes called the 'quilt-as-you-go' technique. I prefer to use a hoop or frame for quilting, as it ensures that all the layers are held evenly and smoothly in place as I quilt. The danger with lap quilting is that the layers will pucker or move in different directions as you gather the work in your lap. By using a hoop or frame, the layers are held evenly and your hands and fingers are freer to concentrate on the quilting. However, this is only personal preference, and many people lap quilt without any problems.

Quilting effects

The quilting stitches compress the three layers of the work together, creating a 'valley' along the line of stitching. The unquilted areas remain puffed up, making 'hills'. As the light catches on the hills, and shadows fall in the valleys of stitching, a pattern of light and dark is created over your patchwork. The patchwork ceases to be two-dimensional and becomes three-dimensional.

You can use quilting simply to highlight the patchwork, or you can create a whole new perspective for the quilt by making the quilting pattern a feature. Areas of plain fabric show off quilting at its best, and often quilts are planned with alternating plain blocks, or areas of plain fabric, to show off a quilting design. Marjorie Coleman's quilt **Macrocarpa** demonstrates this approach.

When you are planning your quilting, try to avoid leaving large areas unquilted. Conversely, if the quilting lines are too close together, the layers will be flattened out.

Some quilting designs

Outline quilting: The simplest form of all is where quilting is used to outline the patchwork or applique shapes. This is particularly effective for applique, as it gives the shapes a slight *bas relief*. Examples of outline quilting can be found in my wallhangings depicting Australian birds and animals.

For pieced designs, quilting can be done 'in the ditch', which means the quilting is as close as possible to the seam line. It can also be just a little distance either side of the seam line. Quilting along the sides of the patches where the seam allowances lie is always more difficult because of the number of layers you have to push the needle through. Sometimes at seam junctions you will find you have to push the need up and through . . . and down and through —a single motion at a time.

Lines: Simple straight lines can create a most effective quilting design. The lines can be parallel, or can create a square or diamond grid. Judy Edwards has used a diamond design in her **Waratah** quilt. Geometric shapes, such as squares, often look best if the quilting goes *across* the diagonal of the patchwork shape. An example of this can be seen in Judy Turner's quilt, **Ashes of Roses**.

Echo quilting: This kind of quilting gets its name because it *echoes* the patchwork or applique shapes, with a series of lines rather like contours on a map. Echo quilting can be seen in the background of the **Turtle, Fish**, and **Crab** cushions.

Motifs and designs: All kinds of shapes and designs can be used as inspiration for quilt designs, from simple circles to complex leaf and flower designs. I find nature is the greatest source for designs of all kinds, such as the design I created for my quilt, **Flannel flower**, which was based on the leaf of the flannel flower. If a motif is to be repeated, transfer the design onto cardboard or plastic, and use these templates to mark your design onto the fabric.

Marking quilting designs

There are three main ways to mark your patchwork for quilting:

Marking with a pencil: This is done *before* the three layers are put together. Use a hard lead pencil that makes a faint line, and spread out the quilt-top on a hard, flat surface.

Lines can be drawn with a ruler, or drawn around cardboard (or plastic) templates of quilting designs. You will find that after you have finished quilting, you will not be able to see these lines, provided they were marked *lightly* to begin with.

You can also use special pens which have ink that vanishes with simple treatment after the line is no longer required. Follow the manufacturer's directions carefully with these pens, and do a pre-test on the fabric before you begin.

Marking with a needle: A large darning needle can be used for drawing lines on your patchwork. Use it like a pencil to scratch lines on the surface of the material. Because the lines do not last long, this marking is done after the three layers are put together, and just before you are ready to quilt. This is a useful technique for marking fabrics with pile, such as velvet.

Marking with masking tape: Strips of masking tape can be laid on the quilt and the straight edges of the tape used as a guide for your quilting. The tape can be used and reused many times, as it will peel off after use and can be restuck on a new section. This method too is employed after the three layers are joined together, just before you are ready to quilt. If necessary, the masking tape can be snipped so it can be eased around curves. You may need to lay the tape alongside a ruler to make straight lines over a long distance.

Preparing for hand quilting

Careful preparation is the secret of successful quilting. It is vital that the three layers of the quilt be smoothly tacked (basted) together, with *no wrinkles* in any of the layers. As I have described already, you can lap quilt small items or parts of a larger quilt, or you can use a hoop or frame for both small or large items. A large frame is really only necessary if you want several people to work on a quilt at once.

Preparation for lap quilting

Step 1
Smooth the pressed backing fabric onto a flat surface such as a table or floor. The right side of the backing should be face down.

Step 2
Lay the batting over the backing, again keeping it smooth.

Step 3
Lay the prepared top over the batting and backing. The top should have been pressed carefully first, as this is be the last time you will be able to iron it. Check that there are no wrinkles.

Step 4
Pin the three layers together, pinning only from above and without putting your hands under the layers, so that the even arrangement of the three layers is not disturbed.

Step 5
Use a tacking thread and a large needle to tack (baste) the three layers together in a grid-pattern over the entire piece. The stitches do not have to be small, but the lines of tacking should be only 10-15 cm (4-6″) apart.

Preparation for quilting in a hoop

Step 1
Prepare the three layers, and tack (baste) them together (as described in *'Preparation for lap quilting'* above). If you are making a large piece, such as a quilt, it is generally unnecessary to pin before you tack, especially if your quilt is spread out on a carpet. If you are working on a smooth surface, such as a wooden floor, it might be necessary to use masking tape to hold the backing in place so that it does not move when you add the other layers.

With a large piece, you may need to make joins in the backing and batting to make them the required size. The pieces of backing can be seamed together on the machine. Join the batting by butting two edges together and, using a large needle and a long thread, loosely stitch the edges together with a whip stitch.

For a large quilt, begin tacking at the centre, and tack out to the four corners, smoothing the quilt out as you go. Then tack (baste) a grid pattern over the whole piece, with lines about 10-20 cm (4-8″) apart. You will need to crawl on top of the quilt to do this.

If you are quilting a small piece, such as a cushion, and still want to use your hoop, make the backing extra large to fit into the hoop. The extra backing can be trimmed off later.

Step 2
Lay the inner hoop down on a flat surface, smooth the quilt over it, and then press the outer hoop over the inner hoop, tightening the hoop to grip the quilt as necessary. The quilt should be smooth in the hoop, but it does *not* need to be drum tight. Make sure there are *no wrinkles* in the area you are about to quilt—at first you might like to keep checking the back of the hoop, but later you will be able to *feel* that the three layers are straight and even.

Begin quilting in the centre of the piece, and always work *from* the section you have quilted towards the unquilted parts, otherwise you will find the layers bunch up between the areas you have quilted.

Preparation for quilting in a frame

Step 1
Prepare the three layers and tack them together as you would for quilting with a hoop.

Step 2
Stitch or pin the backing of the two shorter sides of the quilt to the fabric on the long sides of the frame. If the quilt is large, it is then rolled up to the size of the stretcher bars, and the frame is bolted together. Tapes and pins can be used to stretch the backing fabric to the sides of the frame.

Step 3
Quilting is begun in the centre of the quilt, and as each section is finished, the quilt is unrolled and rerolled to reveal a new area.

The quilting stitch

The quilting stitch is just a running stitch, but it should be as even as possible, and must go through all three layers of the item. Learning it is rather like learning to ride a bicycle—feeling rather awkward in the beginning, but with a little practice, soon mastering it. Don't bother with trying to make the stitches too tiny—the effort is just not worth it. Instead, aim at even stitches. Three to four stitches showing every 2 cm (¾″) is satisfactory.

A thimble is essential for good quilting. Wear it on the middle finger of the hand with which you hold the needle. The thimble should do the work of pushing the needle through. I also like to wear another thimble to protect the pointer finger of my other hand. Some people like to use a leather guard, or cover their finger with sticking plaster.

Use only a short piece of quilting thread, no longer than 45 cm (18″), and tie a knot at the end. Begin by putting the needle through the quilt from the back, coming up exactly on the line you want to quilt. Give a slight tug on the thread to pull the knot through into the batting, then take a small back stitch to secure it. The knot should thus be hidden in the batting.

Pushing the needle with the thimble, stitch down into the quilt until you graze the tip of your pointer finger, which is *underneath* the quilt. Rock the needle back and push upwards so you come out a little way along your quilting line. As you become practised at doing this, you will be able to take more than one stitch at a time. It is necessary to feel the needle with the tip of your finger (or the edge of your second thimble) with each stitch, to know that you have gone through all three layers.

End your quilting with a small back stitch. Then run the thread away into the batting, coming out about 2 cm (¾″) away from the back stitch, and snip off the thread.

You will find it more comfortable to quilt in some directions than others, but if you are quilting with a hoop, or quilting in your lap, you can just move the item about to suit yourself. This is not possible on a large frame, and you may find you have to start and stop more in order to quilt in the direction you wish.

Step-by-step: Quilting by hand

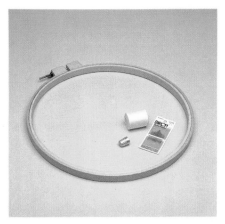

Step 1 Quilting by hand needs some special equipment: quilting hoop, quilting thread, thimble(s), and short needles called 'betweens'.

Step 2 Tack backing, batting, and patchwork top together. Make sure there are no wrinkles. Tack from the centre towards corners first, then add an all-over grid.

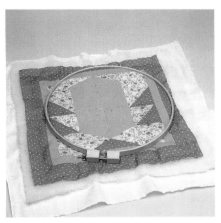

Step 3 Place centre of tacked patchwork in hoop. Make sure that all layers are straight and wrinkle free. Do not pull too tight.

Step 4 With one hand on top and one below, make small running (quilting) stitches. Graze finger below as you stitch, and use the thimble to push the needle.

Step 5 Make your stitches as even as possible. Begin and end with a small back stitch, hiding the starting knot and ending thread in the batting.

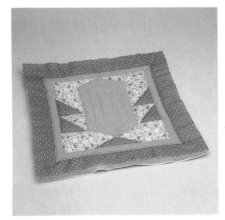

Step 6 The finished quilting of the **Banksia** block. Note it is the shadows formed by the quilting stitches, not the stitches themselves, that make the quilting pattern.

Step-by-step: Strip quilting

Step 1 Cut fabric strips of desired width and length. A roller cutter and mat are very useful with this step.

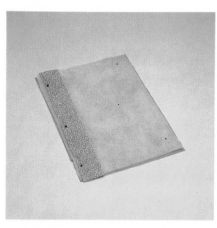

Step 2 Lightly pin batting to backing fabric, then place first strip *right side up* onto prepared layers, and pin in place.

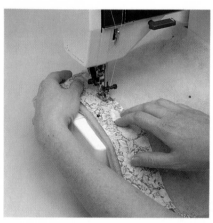

Step 3 Pin second strip on top of first strip, *right side down*. Stitch, making 6 mm (¼″) seam. Fold out second strip and finger press flat.

Step 4 Continue in this manner, adding the number of strips required. Remember to remove pins in batting and backing as you come to them.

Step 5 Edge stitch along the first and last strips. Trim away excess batting and backing around edges.

Step 6 The finished piece of strip quilting, ready to be made up.

Step-by-step: Quilting by machine

Step 1 Set up machine with a large clear space to your left. Add another table if quilting a large quilt. Adjust machine ready for quilting.

Step 2 Spread out backing fabric, then add batting and quilt top. Make sure there are no wrinkles. Pin layers together. Avoid putting pins where quilting lines will go.

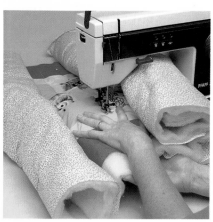

Step 3 Roll the quilt up from both ends. Stitch across centre row, then each row towards edge. Turn the quilt and stitch rows to the other end.

Step 4 Stitch 'in the ditch'. Use your fingers to spread the quilt top sideways each side of the presser foot. Begin and end each row with some back stitches.

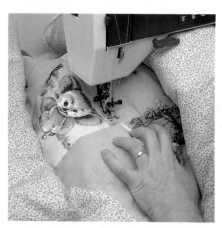

Step 5 Reroll quilt to stitch crosswise rows. To prevent puckering when crossing quilted lines, you may need to stretch the quilt in the direction you are stitching.

Step 6 The finished machine quilting, with batting and backing trimmed ready for binding.

Quilting by machine

Machine quilting is very appealing because of its speed. A complete quilt can be quilted in a matter of days. Machine quilting is also an ideal way to make small items such as cushions, articles of clothing, and cot quilts which will need a lot of washing. However, it is not always as easy as it sounds—it can be tricky getting the three layers to move smoothly through a sewing machine and, with a large quilt, just coping with the bulk can be difficult.

While smaller items will fit through the machine comfortably, large quilts can be machined as a whole (consequently with limitations on the quilting design), or parts of the quilt can be quilted separately and joined together later.

The secret of successful machine quilting is having the three layers move smoothly through the machine together, without one of the fabrics being pushed ahead of the others.

Quilting designs

The line made by the sewing machine is more distinct than the gentle effect of hand quilting, because the machine line is unbroken and also because the stitching tightly compresses the layers together.

Designs for machine quilting should be designs with as few starts and stops as possible.

Machine-quilting designs can be marked as for hand quilting, either by drawing with pencil or special marking pen, or using masking tape as a guide for stitching.

On smaller items, and parts of a quilt, you can quilt any design you wish, turning corners and making small or large curves. However, with whole large quilts, because of the bulk, it is only possible to quilt in straight lines. It is impossible to turn corners when the quilt is all rolled up and travelling through the machine.

Previous pages: Pretty prints skilfully blended together in practical strip-quilted items made by Judy Turner. Complete instructions for strip-quilted cushions are on page 134, and for the travel set, on pages 135-7.

Threads

Threads used for dressmaking are generally suitable for machine quilting and, because they come in a large range of colours, can be closely matched to the patchwork. If there is not an exact colour match, choose a thread that is a shade darker. Match the bobbin thread as closely as possible to the colour of the backing fabric.

You can also use a nylon invisible thread which will blend with all colours, and gives a softer line. This thread is especially useful where you need to quilt over several different colours in one line of stitching. Use the nylon thread on the top only, and put a normal sewing thread on the bobbin (if nylon thread is used on the bobbin, it will snag and tangle).

Backing fabrics

A firm fabric is probably desirable for machine quilting and, although some sheeting is suitable, those with a high polyester content can slip on the lower feed mechanism of the machine, and cause puckering.

For machine quilting, I like to choose a printed backing fabric, as the print hides the starts and stops—especially when there are changes of thread colours. You can also choose a plain colour, and match the thread in the bobbin to it.

Batting

Any batting can be used for machine quilting, but do not use one that is too thick if you are planning to quilt a large quilt in one piece. It will be too bulky to fit through the machine.

Preparing the machine

Step 1
Oil the machine before you start a big project, and make sure the bobbin is full. Check the bobbin from time to time, as it is very annoying to have it run out in the middle of stitching.

Step 2

Set up the machine for flat-bed sewing, if this is possible.

Step 3

Attach your machine's most suitable foot for machine quilting. This will vary from machine to machine—with some machines you use a regular foot, while on others you need to use a zipper, roller, or walking foot. Some machines have dual feed which is especially good for machine quilting. You really need to try some samples of quilting on your machine to find out what works best. Also, consult with a dealer for your particular machine who will suggest what is most suitable.

If you wish to quilt a design that involves turning a lot of corners, choose the machine foot that gives you the *most* visibility ahead of the needle, so that you can follow the marked quilting design.

Step 4

You may need to adjust the stitch length to longer than normal, and perhaps slightly loosen the top tension. On some machines it is also possible to lessen the pressure on the machine foot. Again, try some samples to work out what is best for your particular machine, and the kind of fabrics you are using.

Step 5

Set up a large clear working space for machine quilting. If you are working on a large quilt you will need an L-shaped working area. You can create this by putting your machine on a table (so that there is plenty of space to the left of the machine) and then putting another table (I use a card table) just to your left. This arrangement provides a large flat surface which the quilt can slide along as it moves through the machine.

Preparing for quilting

Step 1

Mark the patchwork top with quilting lines or designs if this is necessary.

Step 2

Spread out the backing, batting and top on a large clear space, such as a carpeted floor. Smooth all layers so there are *no wrinkles*.

Step 3

Pin thoroughly, every 7-10 cm (3-4"), but try to avoid putting pins directly on your stitching lines. Use glass-headed pins, and push them in as far as they will go. Begin pinning at the centre, working only from the top so as not to disarrange the layers. Pin out to the edges, smoothing the quilt as you go. For a large quilt you will need literally hundreds of pins.

Machine quilting small items and parts of quilts

Small items can easily be quilted on the machine, as it is possible to quilt in any direction, making turns and circles. However, it is still advisable, to minimise your starts and stops. For a large quilt, if you want to quilt a design other than one involving straight lines, it is necessary to quilt in small sections and join the parts into a whole quilt later. The resulting seams on the back can be covered with strips of fabric (remember to allow fabric for this in estimating your initial fabric requirements). A piece of approximately a metre (40") square is the largest that can be comfortably put through the machine if turns are to be made. However, larger long thin strips will also work well. It is important to decide how to divide up the quilt for machine quilting when you are planning your quilt, as this will affect your whole construction procedure. The quilt can be quilted block by block . . . or in sections such as quarters or thirds . . . or in strips . . . or medallion fashion working from a centre section out through successive borders.

How to machine quilt

Step 1

Prepare the machine, and pin your patchwork as described above.

Step 2

Begin and end your stitching with several back stitches, or else bring the ends to the back and tie them off later.

Step 3

As the three layers are moving through the machine, use your fingers to spread the piece flat in front of the foot. Use the other hand *underneath* your work to keep the backing flat. With pieced designs, stitch 'in the ditch' (right along the seam line).

It is easiest to sew along the side on which there are no seam allowances, but this is not always possible. If it is necessary to sew along the side where there are seam allowances, it is better to sew just a little out from the fold of the seam, than to try to go too close to the edge and find yourself going off it at times—which results in an unpleasant wiggly line. Applique is most effectively quilted by stitching just outside the applique pieces.

Step 4
Snip off the thread ends neatly, snipping the top thread off first.

Joining pre-quilted sections

When all the sections of the quilt have been quilted, prepare them for joining by trimming back the backing and batting level with the edge of the top, and trimming back the batting to the seam line at all the corners.

Pin the sections together, then sew the seam, sewing through all six layers. Cut away the batting from the seams, and trim the seams. Cover the seams with straight strips of fabric which have been cut 5 cm (2″) wide (note that these are *not* bias strips), with the raw edges folded to the middle and pressed. Pin and hand sew the strips and use them to cover the seams on the back of the quilt.

In cases where the machine quilting *does not come to within 25 mm (1″)* of the sides of the quilted section, an alternative method may be used. Join only five of the six layers together leaving one side of the backing out of the seam. This backing is then folded over and hand stitched on top of the seam to cover it.

Machine quilting a whole quilt

Machine quilting a whole quilt is rather like sewing a two-metre long, limp and uncooperative porcupine! Because of the size of the quilt to be fitted through the machine, the quilting can only be done in straight lines, from one side of the quilt to the other. Diagonal lines are also possible, but again they must go from one side of the quilt to the other. However, you can start the lines from inside a quilt border if you like, and quilt around the border last.

Machine quilting a whole quilt

Step 1
Prepare the quilt as described earlier.

Step 2
Roll up the quilt from each end, exposing only a part of the centre section. The roll on the right side of the centre section should be small enough to fit through the arm of your machine.

Step 3
Handle the quilt gently—it is prickly!

Step 4
Starting from one edge, begin with a couple of back stitches, then sew from one side of the quilt to the other, sliding the right-hand side roll through the arm of the machine as you go. Stitch 'in the ditch' along the seam lines, and finish each line with a couple of back stitches.

Step 5
As you stitch, feed the quilt through with your left hand guiding the quilt under the needle, using your fingers to spread the quilt sideways on each side of the needle. Use your right hand to help push the roll of the quilt under the arm of the machine, and to feel that the backing keeps smooth throughout the procedure.

Step 6
You will probably have to start and stop to manoeuvre the quilt from time to time. Always stop with the needle down through the quilt, as this helps you to keep the lines straight.

Step 7
If the top seems to be bunching, apply more pressure with your hand when flattening the fabric on either side of the needle. This evens out the fullness, and stops the presser foot pushing the top layer ahead of the other two.

Step 8
Continue in this fashion, stitching row after row, and gradually unrolling the part of the quilt going through the arm of the machine. When half of the quilt is finished in this fashion, turn the quilt around so that the next row will again begin at the centre. Now the unquilted half is rolled up and going under the arm of the machine, and the quilted half rolled up and going past the left side of the machine. Gradually work outward to the other edge.

Step 9

As you roll and reroll the quilt, some of the pins will inevitably work themselves loose and fall out. Ignore them and do not try to repin unless the quilt is once again spread out completely flat on the floor.

Step 10

When all the lines going in one direction are completed, reroll the quilt as required to quilt the other lines of the design. For example, if you have begun by doing all the crosswise lines, you will have to reroll the quilt in the other direction to do the lengthwise lines. The second lot of quilting generally seems easier, as the quilt is well held together by the first lines of stitching. However, watch for bunching of the layers as you cross the quilting lines you have already done. If you see a bunch or pucker forming, you can pull the quilt outward in the direction that you are stitching (before, you applied pressure sideways).

Step 11

If your design involves quilting around the border or borders, do this last.

Strip quilting

Strip quilting is a type of machine quilting in which strips of fabric are pieced, backed and quilted in one single operation. It is a one-step way to quick and easy patchwork, and is a technique especially suited for making small items such as bags and purses. It also can be used to make whole quilts, such as Beryl Hodges' **Irish Inspirations**, a quilt which gains its impact from a clever arrangement of tonal contrasts in the strip-quilted blocks.

It is generally preferable to use thin, firm batting for strip quilting, because the thicker, softer batting is more difficult to work with.

Prepare your machine for machine quilting, as described previously (p. 127). It is a good idea to try a small sample to check the stitch length, making adjustments so that the layers move smoothly through the machine.

Doing strip quilting

Step 1
Cut pre-washed and pressed fabric into strips. Strips can be made by using scissors to cut fabric along pencil lines, or else a roller cutter can be used to run along the side of a ruler. The wide clear rulers specially developed for patchwork are very useful for this. The combination of a roller cutter and mat and one of these rulers can make quick work of cutting the strips. The strips are usually cut the same width, and 5 cm (2″) is a good size, but the width can vary as you wish. It is most economical to cut the strips from selvedge to selvedge across the fabric, and use them as required. Any scraps left over when the strip quilting is trimmed can be used on future small projects.

Step 2
Prepare a backing fabric. As strip quilting is a form of machine quilting, you will need a fairly firm backing material. Cut the backing 25 mm (1″) larger than the size of the finished item.

Step 3
Prepare the batting by cutting it 25 mm (1″) larger than the finished item. Lay the batting on top of the backing, and pin them together.

Step 4
Beginning on the left side (though with some projects you may need to begin in the centre), lay a strip of fabric right side *up* on top of the backing and batting.

Step 5
Take another strip of fabric and put it on top of the strip already in place, this time putting the right side *down* (the two right sides will now be together). Pin them in place, and machine stitch down the right-hand edge of the strips, making a 6 mm (¼″) seam. Remove the pins and fold back the strip you have stitched, pressing the seam flat with your finger. (Note that you cannot use the iron once the strips are sewn to the batting—it would fuse and flatten the batting.)

Step 6
Be sure to check the back of each row as it is stitched, to ensure that there are no folds or puckers. It is most inconvenient to discover a problem several rows later, when the only means of correction is to unpick all your previous work. Also, do not forget to remove the pins on the batting and backing before you come to them—you do not want them to be stitched into your strips.

Step 7
Lay your next strip over the one just sewn, right sides together, and stitch and press flat with your fingers as before. Proceed in this manner until you have completely covered the batting and backing.

Step 8
Trim the edges of the piece to the required size. Then stitch along the edges of the outside strips to hold them in place.

Bias strips

Bias strips are frequently used in patchwork to cover raw edges. In some situations it is possible to use *purchased bias binding*, which comes with the seam allowances pressed and folded. Purchased bias binding is described by its width with the seam allowances already folded, and the size most useful for patchwork is 25 mm (1″) wide. However, it is not always possible, or desirable, to use purchased bias binding, so that bias strips must be made from one of your own fabrics. Note that bias strips in this book are measured by the width of the fabric strips, raw edge to raw edge. While the amount of fabric needed to make bias varies with the width of the bias needed, it may be useful to know that 50 cm (20″) of fabric 90 cm (35″) wide will yield approximately 10 m (10½ yds) of 4 cm (1½″) bias. I usually allow an extra metre (40″) of fabric for making bias strips to bind a quilt.

To plan how wide to make your bias strips, you need to first decide how wide you want the finished binding to be when it is seen from one side of the finished article. Double this width, and then add 12 mm (½″) extra, for the seam allowance.

A strong, neat edge is made by making the bias double. Make the bias strips four times the width of the desired finished binding, plus the seam allowances of 12 mm (½″). Join the strips together, then fold and press the bias in half lengthways.

Making bias strips

Step 1
Take a piece of fabric and straighten one of its cut edges along the grain of the fabric. Fold this straightened edge over and align it with one of the selvedge edges. Press this fold, which now gives you a line of true bias.

Step 2
Using a ruler (or previously prepared cardboard strip) mark lines, parallel to the fold line, in the width that you need. Cut along these lines. Alternatively, use the roller cutter, mat and a ruler to cut the fabric.

Step 3
Join the strips together to make the length needed (note that the ends you are joining will actually be on the straight of the grain). Press the joining seams open.

Directions for constructing items

Pot holder

Requirements

- A square of patchwork, about 20 cm (8") in size (plus seam allowance).

  Suggestions: try some simple pieced shapes, such as nine squares 7 cm (2½") in size ... or eight triangles, each made from half of a 10 cm (4") square. You can also use an already prepared square of strip patchwork.

- Two squares of batting 2 cm (¾") larger than your patchwork. (If you are using an already prepared piece of strip quilting, you will only need one square.)

- Two squares of dark-coloured backing fabric prepared the same size as the batting (only one square is needed if you are using already prepared strip quilting).

- Purchased bias binding, 25 mm (1") wide and 1 m (40") long.

- Thread to match the bias binding.

Construction

Step 1
Using one of each of your batting and backing squares, machine quilt around the shapes in your patchwork square. (This step has already been completed if you are using a square of strip quilting.)

Step 2
Lay your second square of backing fabric down, and place the remaining layer of batting over it. Smooth the quilted patchwork on top, and pin all the layers together.

Step 3
Use a wide zigzag stitch around the outside edge of the patchwork, sewing through all the layers (five in all) and slightly rounding the corners as you go. Trim back excess backing and batting to the row of zigzag stitching.

Step 4
Stitching on the wrong side, and making sure that the edge of the patchwork will be *in the centre of the bias* when it is folded over, stitch the bias to the backing side of the pot holder. Begin in one corner, work around the edge of the pot holder, and end by stitching over the bias where you first started—folding the bias over to the right side before you stitch over it. Leave the end of the bias hanging for the loop.

Step 5
Stitch the bias down onto the right side, and stitch the edges of the bias together along the loop section to neaten it. Trim the end of the bias to the size needed for the loop, fold over the raw edge, and form a loop by stitching to the corner of the pot holder.

Tote bag

Requirements

- Two pieces of patchwork, each approximately 40 cm (16") square.

  Suggestions: two squares of simple pieced shapes ... two pieced or appliqued blocks with borders added.

- Two strips of fabric for handles, each 10 cm (4") wide and 46 cm (18") long (or length desired).

- Batting—two squares, 2 cm (¾") larger than patchwork ... and two strips to line handles, each 4 cm (1½") wide and 46 cm (18") long.

- Backing—two squares, same size as batting.

- Lining fabric—two squares the same size as patchwork, plus extra to make pockets, if desired.

- Thread to match lining.

Construction

Step 1

Use the squares of batting and backing to hand or machine quilt the two squares of patchwork. Trim away excess backing and batting.

Step 2

Pin the two quilted squares together, right sides facing. Stitch around three sides of the squares, making a 6 mm (¼″) seam and leaving one side open for the top of the bag. If you want the bag to have a gusset, fold the corners at the bottom of the bag into triangles across the seam, making the base of the triangle the width that you want the gusset of the bag. Stitch across the base of the triangles. Turn the bag right side out.

Step 3

Make the lining. If desired, add pockets to each lining piece. Pin the squares of lining together, right sides facing. Stitch along both sides of the lining squares and partly across the base at each side, leaving a 20 cm (8″) opening at the base. Make these seams 12 mm (½″), so that the lining will be just a little smaller than the bag. If making a bag with a gusset, fold triangles at the corners of the bottom of the lining and stitch, in the same way as you did for the body of the bag. Do *not* turn right side out.

Step 4

Construct the handles. Press over a 6 mm (¼″) seam allowance on both sides of each strip intended for the handles, fold the strips in half lengthwise and press again. Insert the 4 cm (1½″) wide strip of batting into the fold, and stitch along both sides of the handles to hold the batting in place.

Step 5

Pin the handles in place on the outside of the bag, with the handles hanging down, and the raw edges of the handles level with the raw edges of the top of the bag. Stitch the handles in place, with a 6 mm (¼″) seam.

Step 6

Slip the lining over the bag, so that the right sides of the lining are against the right sides of the bag, and the raw edges of both the lining and the body of the bag are even at the top. Pin and stitch, making a 6 mm (¼″) seam. Pull the bag through the hole in the base of the lining. Hand or machine stitch the hole closed.

Step 7

Push the lining into the bag, and sew a row of stitching around the top of the bag to hold the lining in place. You can make this line of stitching nearly invisible if you stitch along the edge of where the border is joined to the block.

Cushion with bound edge

Requirements

- A square of patchwork the size you require the finished cushion to be—40 cm (16″) is a good size.

  Suggestions: use simple geometric shapes pieced together . . . or pieced or appliqued blocks with border strips added . . . or a square of strip quilting.

- Batting 2 cm (¾″) larger than your patchwork. (This will already have been included if you are using a square of strip quilting.)

- Backing fabric for your quilting—the same size as your batting (this will also have already been included if you are using a piece of strip quilting). Because this backing layer will be inside the cushion and will not show, any fabric is suitable.

- Fabric for the back of the cushion, the same width as the patchwork, but 5 cm (2″) longer to allow for the zipper insertion.

- Bias for binding—either 4 cm (1½″) bias strips made of one of the fabrics in the cushion, or purchased bias binding 25 mm (1″) wide. The length will be four times the length of one side of your cushion—2 m (2 yds) should be plenty.

- A zipper 5 cm (2″) shorter than the width of the cushion, and in a colour to match the back of the cushion.

- Thread to match the cushion back.

Facing: **Irish Inspirations** *by Beryl Hodges. Clever use of tonal contrast creates a strong overall design. Detail shows a part of the back of the quilt, to reveal construction techniques. Strip-quilted blocks were joined together, and the seams covered with appliqued strips.*

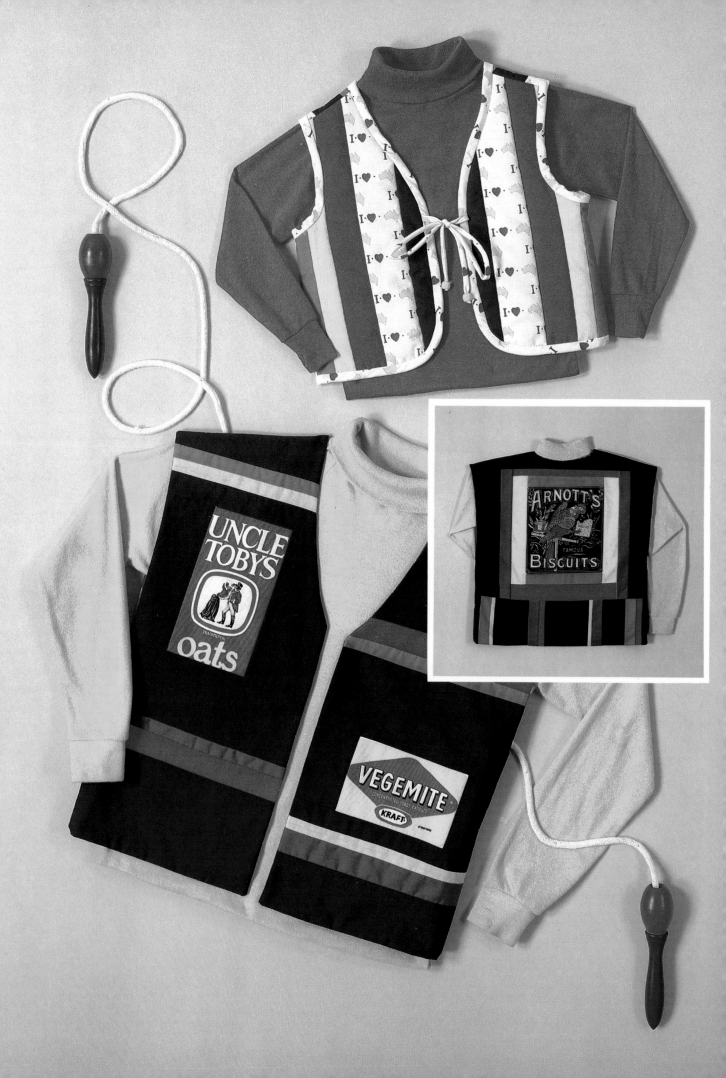

Construction

Step 1

Assemble together the patchwork, batting and backing fabric, and quilt by hand or machine. (This step has already been completed if you are using a square of strip quilting.)

Step 2

Trim edges of backing and batting. To prevent the cushion having pointed 'ears', round off the corners very slightly.

Step 3

Insert the zipper across the centre of the fabric intended for the cushion back, using the extra length you allowed in one direction to make the seam allowances for the zipper.

Step 4

Lay the back of the cushion out flat (with the right side facing down). Cover it with the patchwork top (with its right side facing up). Pin the two together. Note that the seam you are making will be on the *outside* of the cushion.

Step 5

Pin the bias to the cushion on the right side, easing it around the corners. Join the ends of the bias together by pressing folds at the place where it meets. Trim the ends of the bias, leaving a seam allowance past the pressed folds. Then seam the two ends together along the folds. Stitch the bias around the cushion.

Step 6

Fold the bias to the back of the cushion and neatly hand stitch in position.

Facing: Children's vests by Pamela Tawton. A curtain fabric printed with nostalgic Australian labels inspired a colourful vest. Strip quilting was used to make a bright vest for a patriotic pre-schooler. Strip-quilted vest instructions can be found on page 138.

Cushion with frill

Requirements

● Requirements are as for the *'Cushion with bound edge'*, but instead of bias, you need extra fabric for making strips double the width of the required frill with an extra 12 mm (½") for seam allowances ... and six times the length of one side of your cushion (that is, the total length of the frill will be one and a half times the perimeter of the whole cushion).

Construction

Step 1

Construct the cushion as for the *'Cushion with bound edge'* up to the end of *Step 3*. Then proceed according to *Step 2* below.

Step 2

Cut the strips of fabric intended for the frills to the desired width. Join the strips into a circle, fold in half lengthwise, and press.

Step 3

Use four pins to mark the quarters of the circle at the raw edges. Run a double row of gathering stitching between each pair of pins. Pull up the gathers.

Step 4

Place the finished patchwork right side up, and mark the centre of each side with a pin. Place the frill on top of the patchwork, raw edges together. (The frill will be pointing to the centre of the cushion.) Match the marking pins on the frill with the pins at the centre of each of the cushion sides. Pin the frill in place, making sure the gathers are even, and putting some extra gathering at the corners. Stitch the frill in place, using a 6 mm (¼") seam.

Step 5

Keeping the frill neatly pinned out of the way, towards the centre of the cushion, place the right side of the back of the cushion on top of the patchwork and frill. Make sure the *zipper is partly open*, to allow you to turn the cushion right side out later. Pin in place, turn the cushion over, and stitch along the stitching that is holding the frill in place.

Step 6

Turn the cushion right side out through the zipper hole.

Strip-quilted holdall

Requirements

- 18 strips of various fabrics—each strip 5 cm (2″) wide and 92 cm (36″) long.

- Backing fabric, 130 cm (52″) long and 92 cm (36″) wide.

- Batting (the thin firm kind), 120 cm (48″) long and 71 cm (28″) wide.

- Thread to match the backing fabric.

- Zipper, 46 cm (18″) long.

- Purchased bias binding, 25 mm (1″) wide and 2 m (80″) long.

Construction

Step 1

To make the body of the bag, first cut a rectangle of backing and one of batting. Each rectangle is 92 cm (36″) long and 50 cm (20″) wide. Strip quilt the rectangles together—using 13 of the fabric strips, and placing them down the length of the rectangle. Straight stitch the outside edges of the strips, and then trim the backing and batting to these outside edges. (The quilted rectangle should measure approximately 46 cm (18″) *across* the strips.) Trim both the short ends of the rectangle, so that its length is now 88 cm (34½″).

Step 2

To make the gussets for the bag, cut a rectangle of backing and one of batting, each rectangle is 23 cm (9″) wide and 60 cm (24″) long. Strip quilt the rectangles together lengthwise, using five strips of fabric. Straight stitch along the edges of the outside strips, and trim away excess backing and batting to these outside edges. The quilted rectangle should measure approximately 19 cm (7½″) across the strips. Trim the short ends of the rectangle so that its length is 58 cm (23″). Cut this rectangle in half across its length to make the two gussets— each 29 cm (11½″) long.

Step 3

Cut two straight strips of backing fabric, that measure 5 cm (2″) wide and 46 cm (18″) long. Use these strips for binding the short edge of the body of the bag. Fold the strips in half, and stitch them to the backing side of the body of the bag, with all the raw edges together. Fold the binding to the right side, and stitch along the edge.

Step 4

Make the handles. From the backing fabric, cut strips 10 cm (4″) wide and join them to make one strip 254 cm (100″) long. Join the ends of this strip together to make it into a circle. Iron under 6 mm (¼″) on both raw edges, fold in half with the seam allowances towards the inside, and press again. Cut strips of batting 4 cm (1½″) wide, and insert them into the fold of the circle of fabric intended for the handles. Stitch along both sides all the way around the handles, to neaten and hold the batting in place.

Step 5

Join the handles onto the body of the bag. The handles form a loop each side of the bound edges, and should be pinned onto the third strip from the ends of the body of the bag. Pin to within 15 cm (6″) from the bound edges. Position the handles by putting marker pins at the centre of the length of the strips that are third from each end, and use pins to mark the circular handle into halves. Match the pins marking the handle with the pins on the body of the bag, checking at this stage that the handles are even on both sides, and making any necessary adjustments. Stitch the handles in place, stitching over the previous stitching on the handles, and placing a double row of stitching across them 15 cm (6″) from the bound edges of the body of the bag.

Step 6

Insert the zipper. With the zipper closed, pin the zipper under one bound edge, pinning at every second strip. Stitch along one side, stitching along the previous stitching on the binding. You should not need a zipper foot. To finish attaching the zipper, pin and stitch the other side of the zipper in the same manner.

Step 7

Fit gussets into the sides of the bag so that the seams will be on the *inside* of the bag. With the zipper closed, turn the body of the bag inside out and use pins to mark the centre of the gusset at its top and bottom. Pin the gusset to the body of the bag, matching the marking pins and lining up the centre of the top of the gusset with the zipper. Round off the corners very slightly. If the gusset is slightly too large, trim any extra away from the top of the gusset. Stitch from the gusset side, making a 6 mm (¼″) seam, and being careful to stitch the little bit across the zipper from the other side. Repeat for the second gusset. Trim seams neatly.

Step 8
Using the purchased bias binding, cover the raw edges of the seams on the insides of the bag. Machine stitch the bias to the gusset side of the seam. Sew carefully in the area of the zipper. If the zipper is too long, stitch through the zipper several times, both on the seam line and at the very edge of the seam allowance, then cut off any excess zipper. Fold the bias over, and hand stitch down.

Strip-quilted glasses case

Requirements

- Three strips of fabric, 5 cm (2″) wide and 50 cm (20″) long.

- Backing fabric, 15 cm (6″) wide and 50 cm (20″) long.

- Batting (the thin firm kind), same size as backing.

- Purchased bias binding, 25 mm (1″) wide and 80 cm (32″) long—or bias strips, 4 cm (1½″) wide, cut from one of the fabrics.

- Thread to match bias binding.

- A press-stud, or piece of 2 cm (¾″) velcro.

Construction

Step 1
Using the strip-quilting method, strip quilt the three strips of fabric to the backing and batting. Straight stitch along the outside edge of the outer strips. Trim away the backing and batting to the edges of the strips, and trim the length to 47 cm (18½″).

Step 2
Stitch bias across one of the short sides of the rectangle, stitching the bias to the backing side, and making sure that the centre of the bias

will be at the edge of the strip quilting. Fold the bias over and stitch it on the right side.

Step 3
Fold the rectangle over, 20 cm (8″) from the bias-covered edge, and pin.

Step 4
Stitch bias from the fold of the rectangle right around the case, stitching the bias to the side which shows the backing on the flap, and rounding off the corners as you go. Neatly fold the bias at the beginning and end, to cover the raw ends of the bias. Again be careful that the centre of the bias is at the *edge of the strip quilting.*

Step 5
Fold the bias over, and machine stitch along close to the edge.

Step 6
Sew the press-stud or velcro in place to fasten the flap.

Strip-quilted purse

Requirements

- Four strips of fabric, 5 cm (2″) wide and 46 cm (18″) long.

- Backing fabric, 46 cm (18″) wide and 18 cm (7″) long.

- Batting, the same size as backing.

- A zipper, 18 cm (7″) long.

- Purchased bias binding, 25 mm (1″) wide and 50 cm (20″) long—or bias strips 4 cm (1½″) wide, cut from one of the fabrics.

- Thread to match bias.

Construction

Step 1
Strip quilt the four strips along the length of the prepared rectangle of backing and batting. Stitch down the edges of the outside strips, and trim away the extra backing and batting to the edges of the strips. Trim the length of the rectangle to 44 cm (17½″). Cut the rectangle in half, across the strips, to make the two sides of the purse.

Step 2
Insert zip. Leaving the zipper closed, and using a zipper foot on the machine, stitch the zipper face down along the edge of one half of the strip-quilted purse. The right side of the zipper and the right side of the purse are together. Repeat with the other half. To neaten, zigzag the edges of the zipper to the edges of the strip quilting.

Step 3
With right sides facing *outwards*, fold the purse in half at the zipper, and pin. Stitch the purse together around the sides and bottom, opening the zipper slightly so that you can sew close the end of it. Make the seams 6 mm (¼″), and back stitch at the beginning and end to strengthen. Round the corners slightly as you go. Trim away any excess at the corners.

Step 4
Pin the bias around the purse, right sides together. Ease the bias around the rounded corners when pinning. Fold it neatly around the corners near the zipper. Stitch in place. Fold the bias over, and machine stitch close to the edge.

Strip-quilted placemats

Requirements

These requirements make four placemats, each 48 cm (19″) long and 32 cm (12½″) wide.

- Several fabrics—a quantity of 120 cm (48″) by 92 cm (36″) in all.

- Batting (the thin firm kind suitable for strip quilting), 1 metre (40″) long and 71 cm (28″) wide.

- Backing fabric, 1 metre (40″) long.

- Purchased bias binding, 25 mm (1″) wide and 6 metres (7 yds) long.

- Thread to match the bias and backing fabric.

Construction

Step 1
Cut the backing fabric into rectangles, each 2 cm (¾″) larger than the size of the placemats—50 cm (20″) long by 34 cm (14″) wide.

Step 2
Cut the batting into rectangles the same size as the backing.

Step 3
Cut the fabric into strips, 5 cm (2″) wide.

Step 4
Strip quilt the strips to the backing and batting following the general direction for strip quilting (see p. 131). The only variation for these placemats is that the strips are laid across diagonally, and the strip quilting is started in the centre rather than at one side. Lay the first strip diagonally across the middle, from one corner to the opposite corner, and strip quilt out to the edge of the placemat. Turn the mat around, and strip quilt out to the other edge.

Step 5
Make a paper pattern the size of the finished placemat. Measure a rectangle 48 cm (19″) long and 32 cm (12½″) wide. Fold it into four, round off the outside corners, then unfold it. Pin this pattern over your finished rectangle of strip patchwork, and straight stitch around the edge of the paper. Trim back to the edge right next to your straight stitching. Do this for all four mats.

Step 6
Pin the bias around the wrong side of the placemats, beginning with a small fold at the beginning of the bias to make a neat join. Ease the bias around the corners, and make sure that the centre of the bias is *right at the edge* of the strip quilting. Stitch the bias, then fold the bias to the right side of the mat, and machine stitch it in place, to just cover the previous stitching.

Strip-quilted vest

Requirements

- A commercial pattern for a simple vest without darts.

- A selection of fabric for strip quilting, making a total of approximately 50% more than the fabric suggested for the pattern.

- Batting—the amount of fabric suggested for the pattern, plus an extra 10 cm (4″).

- Backing fabric—the same amount as the batting. If desired, a fabric can be chosen that will make the vest reversible.

- Bias strips—either 4 cm (1½″) strips made from one of the fabrics (allow extra fabric for this), or purchased bias binding, 25 mm (1″) wide and the length of the perimeter of the vest, including armholes.

- Thread to match the backing fabric.

Construction

Step 1
Cut out the backing fabric 5 cm (2″) larger all around than the pattern (but do not make larger at the centre back).

Step 2
Cut out the batting the same size as the backing.

Step 3
Pin the backing and batting together lightly, with pins on the batting side.

Step 4
Cut fabric into 5 cm (2″) strips (or width desired), and strip quilt to the backing and batting. The strips can be laid vertically, beginning in the centre of each piece of the vest and working out to the edges (carefully plan the order of your strips to ensure that they match over the shoulders). Alternatively, the strips can be laid in other directions or combinations of directions. First, a block of patchwork or a printed motif could be stitched onto the centre of the back, then strip quilting added around it.

Step 5
Pin parts of the vest together, and try it on to check the fit. Compare with the original pattern if necessary. Trim to the required size.

Step 6
Join the side and shoulder seams, making seams on the wrong sides and sewing through all layers at once. Trim seams, and trim away the batting from the seam allowances. Cut strips of straight fabric 4 cm (1½″) wide from the backing fabric, and press under a small seam allowance on each side of the strips. Pin strips over the seam allowances of the vest, and hand stitch in place.

Step 7
Using bias strips or purchased bias binding, bind all the outside raw edges of the vest. Stitch the bias to the outside of the vest, fold it over and hand stitch to the inside.

Patchwork applied to clothing

There are many possibilities in the application of patchwork to clothing. An example is Linda McGuire's skirt—the pieced **Banksia** block is used to make a border pattern.

Your first step should be to look for a commercial clothing pattern which has an area suitable for the application of patchwork. Look for simple patterns, with no darts or shaping through the area where you wish to place the patchwork. Suitable areas for patchwork can be yokes, bibs, borders, cuffs, pockets, and the centre back (if there is no shaping). Make a pattern of the area on which you wish to use the patchwork, and then construct the patchwork, trimming it (if necessary) to fit your pattern piece. If quilting is involved, remember that the thickness of the quilting may change the fit of the garment, so be sure to make adjustments accordingly.

Quilt construction

Construction procedures are the same for making quilts and wallhangings of all sizes, from small cot quilts to large king-size quilts. Wallhangings are just quilts of any size which hang on the wall rather than cover a bed.

Planning your quilt

Quilt size

The most important first step in constructing a quilt is to determine the finished size of the quilt. For a wallhanging, the size is fairly flexible, but if you want your quilt to fit a particular bed, you should make careful measurements of the size of the bed, and how far the top of the bed is from the floor. Plan how much you want the quilt to hang down—for instance, do you want it to reach almost to the floor, or just to cover the mattress so you can have a bed ruffle as well? The process of quilting causes the patchwork to become slightly smaller so allow some extra for this.

Quilt design

Decide on your block or patchwork design, and how it will be incorporated into the overall quilt. There are many possibilities, and below is a list of examples to be found in this book.

- **Ashes of Roses** by Judy Turner
  Repeating simple shapes.

- **Irish Inspirations** by Beryl Hodges
  Setting blocks next to each other.

- **Flannel flower** quilt
  Alternating blocks of patchwork with blocks of plain fabric.

- **Australian birds** wallhanging
  Setting blocks together with strips between them.

- **Australian wildflowers** quilt
  Setting blocks on the diagonal.

- **Waratah** quilt by Judy Edwards
  and **Sturt's desert pea** quilt
  Medallion design, successive borders surround a central panel.

Adapting the design to the quilt size

Your quilt design may need to be adapted to suit the size you want. There are four main ways of doing this:

- Increasing or decreasing the number of blocks you use.

- Adding borders of various widths. This is one of the easiest ways of changing the quilt size, and also allows a certain amount of flexibility with the size because, if necessary, you can trim back the last border just before you finish the quilt.

- If the quilt design has strips between the blocks, the width of these strips can be increased or decreased.

- Changing the size of the blocks.

Drawing a plan

It is a good idea to draw a plan of the finished quilt. Using graph paper makes this job easier. This plan becomes your blueprint for quilt construction. Of course things may change as your proceed, and you will need to adapt accordingly, but the plan at least gives you a good starting point.

Quilting technique

Decide which quilting technique you are going to use, because this may affect your quilt construction. For instance, if you are planning to machine quilt in sections, you need to decide how best to divide the quilt into convenient parts.

Estimating fabric requirements

There are no really easy short-cuts to estimating fabric requirements, as every quilt is different in its size and pattern. Obviously, the more small pieces there are in a pattern, the more fabric you will lose in seam allowances. The only way to accurately estimate fabric requirements in patchwork is to take some care and consideration. First, make your templates, then count the number of times that each shape will be repeated in your quilt. Take each template shape and find out how many times it will go across the fabric you have chosen (this will vary with the width of the fabric) and then work out how many rows of that size will be needed to make the total number of patches of that shape needed for your quilt. Repeat this procedure for all the template shapes and each fabric required.

When planning a quilt with strips between the blocks, or with borders, it is a good idea to work out how much fabric is needed for these first, as they need to be cut from the whole length of material. After you have worked out the requirements for the strips and/or borders, calculate what is needed for the other patchwork pieces. Do not forget to allow extra fabric for making binding if you are planning to use binding as a finish—you will need an extra metre of fabric to bind a quilt.

Always *overestimate* your requirements, as it is disastrous to run out before your project is completed, and find that the fabric you need is out of stock.

Requirements for backing fabric and batting can be easily estimated from the measurement of your finished quilt, plus an extra 5-10 cm (2-4″) all around for both batting and backing.

Assembling the quilt

The steps described below provide a basic outline of the procedures for making a quilt. For more specific instructions about many of these steps, refer to the earlier chapters on 'Making templates', 'Piecing' and 'Quilting'.

The steps in assembling a quilt

Step 1
Make the templates required (it is a good idea to make a sample block at this point, to check your templates).

Step 2
Mark the fabric, and then cut out the pieces as required.

Step 3
Sew all the pieces together, and assemble the quilt top. If your quilt has multiple blocks, check that they are all square and the same size before you begin joining them together. Work always from small units to larger units. For instance, if you are making a quilt with repeated blocks, first construct the blocks, then stitch the blocks into rows, and finally stitch the rows together.

If the blocks are separated by strips, sew short strips between the blocks to make rows, then put long strips between each of the rows as you stitch the rows together. Before you stitch the strips, mark on them the intervals where the blocks will go and pin accordingly—this ensures that your quilt does not become crooked.

For medallion-style construction, begin with the centre section of your quilt, then add borders or other blocks to make the design. Always measure your borders carefully before adding them—don't just stitch them on, as this will stretch the border fabric and will result in borders that will not hang nicely.

Step 4
Press the top well. Remember this is the last chance you will have to do this.

Step 5
If necessary, mark your quilting design.

Step 6
Prepare the backing fabric, making it 5-10 cm (2-4″) larger than the finished patchwork.

Step 7
Prepare the batting, making it as large as the backing. If necessary, join the batting by butting two edges and zigzagging them together by hand.

Step 8
Spread the quilt, or quilt sections, on a large surface and prepare them for quilting.

Step 9
Quilt by hand or machine. Trim the edges of the quilt back to the patchwork.

Step 10
Finish the edges. There are three main ways of finishing edges:

- *Covering the edge with binding.* Strips to make binding can be cut on the straight grain of the fabric, or can be bias strips—the latter will be necessary if you want the binding to curve around corners. If possible, make the binding strip double—see 'Bias strips' (p. 132).

  Measure the binding so that it will be the right length for the quilt. This is an important step to ensure that the binding is not too loose as it is sewn onto the quilt. (If the binding is too loose, it results in an unpleasant wavy edge.) Pin the binding around the quilt, putting it on the right side of the quilt. Place the binding so that, when it is stitched, the edge of the quilt comes right to the centre of the binding. Machine stitch the binding in place. Fold the binding over to the back of the quilt. Pin it and hand stitch.

- *Overlapping the front to the back.* Bring the last fabric of the quilt top (usually a border) to the back, fold under a small seam allowance, and hand stitch in place. (Alternatively, the backing fabric can be brought to the front.)

- *Stitching the edges of the top and backing together.* Fold under a small seam allowance on both the top and the backing. Trim the batting back to the fold. Hand stitch the top and backing together with two rows of stitching, one close to the edge, and another a little way inside the front row.

Step 11
Sign and date the back. The quilt you make today will become an heirloom tomorrow—don't let it become anonymous.

'Australian birds' wallhanging

Requirements

- Fabric for applique blocks. You will need a wide assortment of small pieces of fabric in different colours (both prints and plains) including 80 cm (32″) pale blue fabric for sky backgrounds. Spotted fabrics can be useful for eyes. A small piece of *lightweight* iron-on vilene may be needed to back some of the lighter fabrics.

- Fabric for strips and a border—the original had 25 mm (1″) wide strips between the blocks and a 75 mm (3″) border, so a piece 30 cm long and 110 cm wide (12″ x 44″) is needed for the strips, and a piece 40 cm wide and 120 cm long (16″ x 48″) is needed for the border.

- Backing fabric—a soft lawn is suitable, 120 cm (48″) square.

- Batting—120 cm (48″) square.

- Threads—sewing threads to match the coloured fabrics, and white quilting thread.

Construction

Follow the general instructions as in 'The steps in assembling a quilt' (p. 141).
Step 1
All patterns are based on a 30 cm (12″) square. You will need to make background squares this size, plus 6 mm (¼″) all around seams. Join two fabrics together by machine to make horizons, where this is needed.

Step 2
To make the block, follow the general instructions for applique (p. 60), noting the following special circumstances:

- Spotted fabrics can be used for the eyes of the **Black swan, Galah, Emu** and **Pelican.** Follow the instructions for making applique circles (p. 61).

- A reverse applique technique (p. 61) is used to make the white feathers on the **Black swan's** wing, and the holes in the trees for the **Cockatoo, Galah** and **Kookaburra.**

- If the background shows through the white fabric used on the **Cockatoo** and **Pelican,** use vilene to back it. Use the vilene only on the shapes, and *not* on the seam allowances.

- Make the narrow birds claws with strips cut on the bias (p. 61).

- Put a small white stitch on the eyes of the **Superb blue wren** and the **Kookaburra** as a highlight.

- To make the stripe on the **Black swan's** beak, machine sew a very narrow strip of white fabric between two pieces of red fabric, pressing the seams toward the red. Place this on the tracing paper pattern of the beak, putting the stripe in the correct place, and cut out the beak. Don't worry about matching the grain in this situation.

Step 3

Cut strips:
- 4 pieces 37 mm wide and 1012 mm long (1½″ x 40½″)
- 12 pieces 37 mm wide and 312 mm long (1½″ x 12½″)

These measurements include 6 mm (¼″) seams.

Step 4

Assemble the top by joining the blocks together into rows of three, with short strips between each block and strips at the beginning and end. Then join these rows together with the longer strips between, and at the top and bottom.

Step 5

Add the outside border. Cut strips 12 cm (5″) wide and the length required as measured against the finished piece, pin carefully and sew to the sides, making mitred corners.

To mitre corners: Sew border strips to the edge of the piece, but *do not* sew into the seam allowance at the corners—begin and end with a few back stitches just before the corners. Mark a 45° angle on the two pieces at each corner, pin together and stitch, again being careful not to stitch into the seam allowance. Trim the seams and press these seams open.

Step 6

Assemble the layers ready for quilting, and hand quilt as described in the section on *'Quilting by hand'* (p. 124). Quilt around each bird and all other shapes you wish to stand out in slight bas relief. Some quilting lines are suggested on the designs by broken lines—such as down the centre of the gum leaves, and a pattern of ripples around the **Black swan**. Quilt around the inside of each square, and around the inside edge of the border.

Step 7

Finish the wallhanging by trimming the backing and batting to the required size, then turn the edge of the border to the back, turn under a small seam allowance and hem down.

'Australian wildflowers' quilt

Requirements

- Fabric for applique. You need a wide assortment of small pieces of fabric in different colours for making the applique flowers. Mostly you will need plain-coloured fabrics, but some prints can be used effectively. For instance a red fabric with small white dots can be used for the **Bottlebrush** and **Red flowering gum**. A small piece of *lightweight* iron-on vilene may be needed for backing pale colours.

- Fabrics for background, strips and borders
  - 4.5 m (5 yds) of 110 cm (45″) light-coloured fabric, for the background blocks and a 5 cm (2″) border.
  - 4 m (4½ yds) of darker fabric, to make 5 cm (2″) wide strips, and two borders—one 5 cm (2″) and another 10 cm (4″). Included in this is extra fabric to make the binding for the edge of the quilt.

- Batting—225 cm (90″) wide and 275 cm (110″) long.

- Backing—the same size as the batting. A soft lawn is suitable.

- Threads—colours to match the fabrics for applique, and white quilting thread.

Construction

Follow the general instructions for *'The steps in assembling a quilt'* (p. 141).

Remember the applique designs fit into a 30 cm (12″) square *set on the diagonal* (if you want to put the designs on squares set straight, you will need 36 cm (14″) square blocks, and extra fabric will be required).

Step 1

Make cardboard templates the shape of your full, half and quarter blocks, adding an extra 6 mm (¼″) all around for the seam allowance. First, cut out the border strips of your light-coloured fabric, then mark and cut out the blocks (with the grain running vertically through the block). The sides of the blocks will be on the bias, but the outside edges of the part-blocks will be on the straight.

Step 2

Applique the blocks, following the general instructions for applique (p. 60). Note the following special circumstances:

- Light coloured fabrics used for **Giant waterlily** and **Sturt's desert rose** may need to be backed with iron-on vilene so that the background does not show. Use the vilene only on the shape, and not on the seam allowance.

- Follow the instructions for making circles (p. 61) for making the **Golden wattle** block. Only two sizes of circles need to be made, one a little smaller than the other (originally a one cent and two cent coin were used to make the circles). Varying the direction of the grain of the circles can give a richer effect.

- Reverse applique (p. 61) can be used for the centres of **Red flowering gum**, **Everlasting daisy** and **Royal bluebell**.

- To make the blocks which involve a lot of small pieces, such as **Pink Heath** and **Tea-tree**, first tack (baste) the stems in place. All the other details can then be added over the top.

- Many of the flowers and leaves have zigzag edges (p. 61).

Step 3

From the darker fabric, cut strips and borders the required length and width, remembering to add a 6 mm (¼″) all around. Cut the strips on the straight grain of the fabric. Mark the strips at the intervals where the blocks will go. It is very important to mark in this way, as the sides of the blocks are on the bias, and will be inclined to stretch. The sides of the blocks must be carefully pinned to the strips, and any fullness of the bias sides eased to fit the marked strips.

Step 4

Join the blocks together into rows, with the strips between. Then join the rows together, again with strips between.

Step 5

Add borders, measuring and pinning before you sew to avoid stretching (be very careful not to stretch the outside ends of the strips which are on the bias).

Step 6

Assemble the three layers together and prepare them for hand quilting (p. 125). Quilt around around each flower and, if desired, quilt a background pattern of lines echoing the shape of the block. Quilt around the inside of each block, and along both sides of the lighter border strip.

Step 7

Finish the quilt with bias binding strips. Cut strips 9 cm (3½″) wide to make doubled bias strips.

'Australian animals' wallhanging

Requirements

- An assortment of plain and print fabrics in natural colours, for applique shapes and background blocks.

- 1 m (40″) of fabric for strips and binding.

- 50 cm (20″) of fabric for border.

- Batting, 80 cm (32″) wide and 120 cm (48″) long.

- Backing, same size as batting.

- Threads—to match coloured fabrics for applique, and white quilting thread.

Construction

Step 1

Make the six applique blocks following the general directions for applique (p. 60). The designs have been drawn *full size* to fit background blocks 20 cm (8″) wide and 24 cm (9½″) long, not including seam allowances. Small details such as eyes and noses can be appliqued using fine closely-woven cotton fabric (do not worry about matching the grain for these small pieces). Alternatively, these details can be embroidered in satin stitch. Note the following special circumstances:

- For **Koala**, applique the tree branches first, and add the koala on top. Make eyes according to the directions for making circles, and make toes following the method for making zigzags (p. 61).

- For **Wombat**, make a separate piece for the left ear, and lay it behind the main body shape.

- For **Echidna**, make the body shape according to the directions for making zigzag edges (p. 61). Place the body shape down first, and lay the foreground over this. Make the claws from narrow bits of fabric on the bias.

- For **Kangaroo**, applique the bush shape first. Place the left foreleg and hindleg behind the body shape and then put right hindleg, foreleg and face over the top.

- For **Platypus**, make the body shape first and put the webbed feet and bill on top.

- For **Possum**, make the body shape first, cutting out the entire silhouette including the ears. Carefully tack down the centre of the tail, to hold the spiral in place. Put the branch on top of the body, adding inside ears, eye, nose and claws last. Claws can be made from narrow bits of fabric on the bias.

Step 2
Cut out strips and borders. Strips between blocks are 4 cm (1½″) wide, plus 6 mm (¼″) all around for seam allowances. Border strips are 8 cm (3″) wide plus seam allowances.

Step 3
Following the general directions for quilt construction (p. 140), assemble the quilt top, and prepare the three layers for quilting.

Step 4
Hand quilt around each shape, and around the edge of each block and border.

Step 5
Bind the outside edge with binding made from strips cut 6 cm (2½″) wide. Fold and press these strips in half lengthways, and use them double.

'Flora Australiana' stained-glass wallhanging

Designed by Pamela Tawton

Requirements

- Assortment of plain coloured fabrics for the flowers.

- Fabric for blue backgrounds—1 m (40″) each of pale blue and ice blue, and 50 cm (20″) of very pale blue. (*Note:* there are three shades of blue, each a little lighter than the other).

- 2 m (80″) of black lawn for bias strips.

- 1.5 m (60″) of black fabric, for strips between the blocks and for a border.

- White lawn for backing blocks, 2.5 m (3 yds).

- Black sewing thread.

Construction

Step 1
Make the nine blocks, following the instructions for bias applique (p. 110).

Step 2
Cut the black fabric into strips 72 mm (3″) wide—this includes 6 mm (¼″) seam allowances, and the required length. Sew the blocks together with strips between, and add a border around the outside.

Step 3
Finish as desired. The original was stretched onto a wooden frame, and a decorative wooden frame added around the outside. Alternatively, to make a soft wallhanging, you could add an extra fabric border to the outside, and quilt it.

The final word

Patchwork has a long tradition in England and America, and also has been done in Australia since early colonial times. However, this book is not about the past—it is a book written, I hope, for the present and future. While the book draws on past tradition (especially the American tradition) for techniques, the aim is to inspire people to use those techniques to make patchwork that is truly Australian. I believe that meaningful evolution in craft occurs when old ways are adapted to new environments and materials. We as Australians are becoming increasingly aware of ourselves, and our unique and beautiful environment. Why not express this awareness through the craft of patchwork?

As for the designs themselves, I am frequently asked if I mind when people make changes to them. My reply is always that I am *delighted* if my designs are altered. I offer these designs as a starting point, hoping that they will be used and adapted to create something new—and something Australian.

Margaret Rolfe

Index

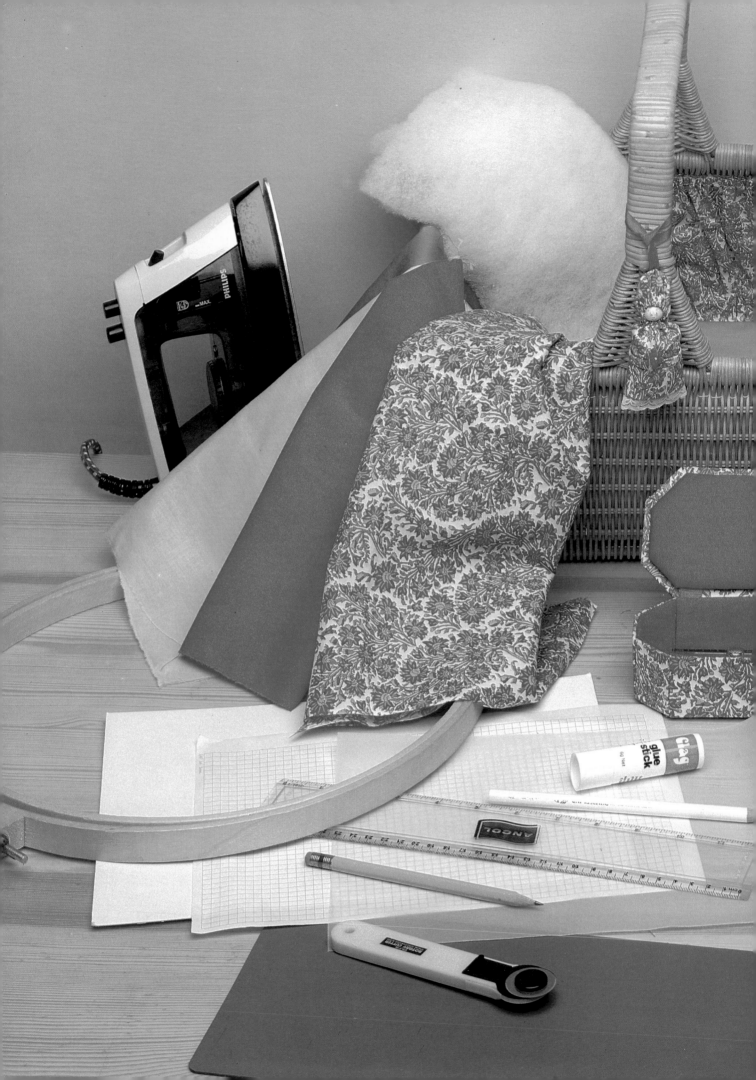